When a scientist of the distinction of Professor Jacques Monod, Nobel Prize winner, Director of the Pasteur Institute in Paris, and one of the world's most able molecular biologists, turns his attention (in his book, *Chance and Necessity*) to the implications of his discoveries for man, his conclusions demand the fullest consideration. No one can question his authority in his own field or his complete integrity in developing the implications of his views; but one may be permitted to extend the same caution that he has enjoined on "a number of very able scientists who have not applied in other fields the same competence that they would exert in their own". (Jacques Monod, in a BBC broadcast.) In other words, criticism, the very distinguished contributors believe, must not be silent when Professor Monod links his scientific theories with his metaphysical convictions and declares, in professed Cartesian terms, that . . .

> "*. . . anything can be reduced to simple, obvious, mechanical interactions. The cell is a machine. The animal is a machine. Man is a machine.*"

This form of materialism has resulted in a tendency to reduce biology to physics, the person to instinct and conditioned behaviour, and minds to machines; views which lead to, or support, particular types of philosophical and sociological conclusions concerning the nature and fate of humanity, which if widely accepted, would both reflect and help to induce a feeling of despair concerning the fate and direction of humanity. One combats this "nothing but" philosophy not by attempting to exempt life and mind from the laws of nature, but by producing, on new premises, a more adequate and comprehensive view of science, of nature, and of man—a non-dualistic conception which, however, is *not* reductive.

It is the authors' conviction that to pass beyond reductive materialism, to renew one's conception of nature as living, and to see people once more as living beings in a world of living beings, constitutes the major task of philosophy today. In assembling the contributions for this important book, John Lewis has been fortunate in securing the co-operation of some of the most distinguished minds in the sciences involved and in that philosophy which seeks to understand the relations of science to man and his destiny.

THE TEILHARD STUDY LIBRARY

SCIENCE AND FAITH IN TEILHARD DE CHARDIN
Claude Cuénot, with a Comment by Roger Garaudy

EVOLUTION, MARXISM AND CHRISTIANITY
Claude Cuénot, F. G. Elliott, R. Garaudy, Bernard Towers and A. O. Dyson

ENERGY IN EVOLUTION
John O'Manique

NAKED APE OR HOMO SAPIENS?
John Lewis and Bernard Towers

CHINA AND THE WEST: MANKIND EVOLVING
Robert Jungk, Ernan McMullin, Joseph Needham, Joan Robinson, Stuart Schram, William G. Sewell and Bernard Towers

HOPE AND THE FUTURE OF MAN
Carl Braaten, John B. Cobb, Lewis S. Ford, Donald P. Gray, Philip Hefner, Johannes B. Metz, Jurgen Moltmann, Christopher F. Mooney, Schubert M. Ogden, Wolfhart Pannenberg, Joseph Sittler and Daniel Day Williams. Edited by Ewert H. Cousins

Edited by John Lewis

# Beyond Chance and Necessity

*A Critical Inquiry into Professor Jacques Monod's Chance and Necessity*

*Contributors*
David Bohm Theodosius Dobzhansky
Arthur Koestler John Lewis Robin E. Monro
Joseph Needham Arthur Peacocke Owen St. John
W. H. Thorpe C. H. Waddington Mary Warnock

GARNSTONE PRESS

Published by
THE GARNSTONE PRESS LIMITED
59 Brompton Road, London SW3 1DS

ISBN 0 85511 181 X

Printed by Cox & Wyman Ltd, London, Fakenham and Reading

S. 1

Philosophy

also studied secretarial and
‹shire Post but, I didn't feel as
so I left to go on and train

MAY 1993 JUNE 1994

. pass my typing exams

SEPT 1994 PRESENT DAY

*Acknowledgments*

Grateful acknowledgments are made to the authors and publishers from whose works contributions to this symposium have been made: to Dr. Joseph Needham for an extract from his Herbert Spencer Lecture on *Integrative Levels and the Idea of Progress*, to Mr. Arthur Koestler for an abridgement of *Beyond Atomism and Holism*, from the Alpbach Symposium of which he was the Editor, and to his publishers, Messrs. Hutchinson; and to Mrs. Mary Warnock and the Editor of the *Listener* for her review of *Chance and Necessity*.

# CONTENTS

## *Foreword*

When a scientist of the distinction of Professor Jacques Monod, Nobel Prize winner, Director of the Pasteur Institute in Paris, and one of the world's most able molecular biologists, turns his attention to the implications of his discoveries for man, his conclusions demand the fullest consideration. No one can question his authority in his own field or his complete integrity in developing his views, but one may be permitted to extend to the development of his inquiries into other departments than those in which he is well versed, the caution that he himself has enjoined on . . .

> ". . . a number of very able scientists who have not applied to some themes in which they have become interested the same strict standards of reasoning that they invariably follow in their own professional work."[1]

In other words, criticism must not be silent when Professor Monod follows his scientific statements with metaphysical speculations extending far beyond molecular biology, and declares, in professed Cartesian terms, that . . .

> ". . . anything can be reduced to simple, obvious, mechanical interactions. The cell is a machine; the animal is a machine; man is a machine."[1]

This form of materialism has resulted in a tendency to reduce biology to physics, the person to instinct and conditioned behaviour, and minds to machines—views which, if widely accepted, lead to philosophical and sociological conclusions concerning the fate and direction of humanity which cannot but induce despair for the future of mankind. We combat

[1] Quotations from Professor Monod's BBC lecture.

this "nothing but" philosophy not by attempting to exempt life and mind from the laws of nature, but by producing, on new premises, a more adequate and comprehensive view of science, of nature, and of man—a non-dualistic conception which, however, is not reductive.

In assembling the contributions for this symposium I have been fortunate in securing the co-operation of contributors not only distinguished in the sciences involved in these discussions, but also in the philosophy which seeks to understand the relations of science to the wider spheres and to man's unique place in nature.

Professor Thorpe raises, in his introduction, the fundamental issue of the validity of interpreting higher levels of biological organisation in terms of the lower levels; Mrs. Mary Warnock introduces our critique with a wide reaching and witty review of Professor Monod's book *Chance and Necessity*,[2] raising in particular the questions of the grounds of his rationalism and the basis of his moral ideals and values. Dr. Arthur Peacocke, a participant in the television discussions with Monod, raises the question of whether Nature and Man, contemplated as a whole, do not reveal purpose and progress in their history without that implying any animistic intrusion into the operations of natural law. Dr. Owen St. John and I take up the general question of the Cartesian materialism which Monod professes and the philosophical difficulties in which that position involves us. We follow with a restatement of the organismic theory in its more modern form. This theme is taken up by the contributions of Dr. Joseph Needham and Mr. Arthur Koestler. Dr. Needham will make it plain that the objections which Professor Monod raises to organicism were effectively dealt with many years ago; Mr. Arthur Koestler further elucidates this position. Their exposition should make it clear that evolution and the appearance of life and mind do not require the intrusion of a "life force" operating upon inanimate matter. While so far we have not challenged any of the positions of Professor Monod on his own ground, molecular biology and genetics, but only on his excursions into alien fields, Professor Waddington, as a geneticist and evolutionist, contributes his own most recent investigations and conclusions, which in many points diverge from those of Professor Monod. Dr. Robin Monro, a distinguished Cambridge molecular biologist, goes even further in questioning some of the basic theories in *Chance and Necessity*, and showing how this invalidates many of Monod's conclusions. Professor David Bohm returns to the question

[2] Alfred Knopf, New York, 1971; William Collins, London, 1972.

raised at the beginning by Mrs. Warnock as to the grounds of rationality, which, for Professor Monod, appear to take the form of existentialist commitment. Finally Professor Dobzhansky, perhaps the most authoritative worker in the field of genetics of human evolution, contrasts the world view of the mechanistic materialist with that of the emergent evolutionist. Of course the contributors are responsible only for their own chapters and are in no way committed to the views expressed in any of the others.

It is our conviction that to pass beyond reductive materialism, to renew our conception of nature as living, and to see ourselves as living beings in a world of living beings, constitutes the major task of philosophy today.

JOHN LEWIS
*Editor*

CHAPTER ONE

# Introduction

W. H. THORPE

During the last few years those who have tried to keep abreast of developments in the general outlook of science and scientists, particularly biologists, will have been gradually gaining the impression that one of the key problems of the present day in biology is posed by "Reductionism". How far is the living world, as we now understand it, capable of complete explanation and description in terms of the non-living components with which the physicists and chemists deal? And to come to the highest levels of biology, namely to Man himself and what appear to be his nearest relatives, the apes, again the question is raised—how far is there a real gap, a real discontinuity, between the mental organisation of apes and of man? If we go back to primitive cultures and try to understand the attitude of primitive peoples to the world around them, it is generally fairly obvious that they regard the world as in some sense a single unit, a real "universe". That is to say, primitive man tends to personalise the whole of his environment, animate and inanimate, and to explain everything he does not understand in terms of spirits, gods, devils and the like. This is, of course, what is meant by animism. Rocks and trees, streams and wells, flowers, lightning and the stars are all regarded as the expression of mentalities; beneficent, neutral or malevolent as the case may be. The scientific method is, of course, a complete breakaway from this in that it entails the focusing of attention on small parts of the whole; thus beginning the process of analysis into discrete objects, discrete fragments or discrete tendencies. When physics arrived at a reasonably satisfactory concept of atoms, it began to be widely felt that the atomic underpinning of things must have greater reality than things directly observed; for if everything is made up of atoms surely, in some sense, atoms must be the very essence of the physical world. This undoubtedly provided strong reasons for the attempt in the reductionist philosophy to explain everything in terms of atoms. And so we have one rather extreme modern definition of the term "reductionism" as *"the attribution of reality exclusively to the smallest constituents of the world and the tendency to interpret higher levels of organisation in terms of lower levels"*.[1] If now we come to find this process scientifically or philosophically unsatisfactory then we have to show that at least many complex macroscopic structures are as basic in some ways as the atomic substructures. If we find, as indeed we do find, that this process is incomplete and unsatisfactory as a general methodology of science then we come to realise that besides this process of analysis, we must all the time maintain the opposite process of synthesis; for without these two together all our activities are likely to be partial and limited in their results. The fact of the matter is that the analytical thinking which underlies reductionism is itself an abstraction from the more elaborate and complex reality.

At first sight all this might seem to be very academic and of slight interest to the ordinary man and woman. But that is a misunderstanding. A few years ago Sir Alistair Hardy remarked that he could only regard the present day reductionist or monistic views of so many scientists and humanists as exceedingly dangerous for the future of civilisation, in that it tends to regard a man's spiritual side as simply a superficial by-product of a material process; for naturally, if it is found that reductionism is a full and sufficient technique for interpreting all material things, then every effort will be made by the thorough-going reductionist, the dedicated reductionist, to explain every aspect of our experience in the same way, namely as *nothing more* than materialism.

The problem has been recently brought to the fore once again by the publication in France of a book by Jacques Monod entitled in the English translation *Chance and Necessity*, but with the subtitle "An Essay on the Natural Philosophy of Modern Biology". It is this subtitle which really raises the main issue. As a biologist Monod has achieved great fame; including the Nobel Prize for his work on messenger RNA. That is to say he is a molecular biologist of very great distinction who has made an outstanding contribution to a particularly active and important field at the present time. There is no doubt that he is a genuine seeker after truth, brave (as his activities during the Resistance showed), deeply concerned about the welfare of the human race, extremely

[1] Barbour, I. G. (1966) *Current Issues in Science and Religion*, p. 52.

intelligent and alert. He is also a first class musician to whom the musical art means a very great deal. He has recently become Director of the Pasteur Institute. So within his field he rightly has the almost universal respect of his biological colleagues. I should however also add that being a good molecular biologist does not *necessarily* confer a comprehensive view of science; and indeed Monod has not infrequently made statements, both in his own country and elsewhere, which have led many biologists to conclude that he regards molecular biology and biological chemistry as the essence of the subject and that henceforth it did not matter if research in all other branches of biology Genetics, Ecology, Behaviour, etc., were allowed to run down. This naturally does not please students and research workers in these and many other branches of science and has given rise to some vigorous hostility—especially in France. And the very fact that Monod has on occasion taken this view (though he now seems somewhat more cautious) shows how strongly he is attracted by a completely reductionist programme. He appears to think that he has found the physico-chemical basis of life, and therefore has shown the way to understand, interpret and control the whole of the living world. So it is not surprising when we read his book to find besides an immensely able and readable summary of his own field of molecular biology a number of statements which imply extreme reductionism.

But although the book contains as vigorous and aggressive reductionist statements as one can find anywhere, once he gets outside his own speciality and starts to discuss what he considers to be the natural philosophy of biology we encounter a morass of undefined terms, contradictory statements and misleading rhetoric. Although he stigmatises all those who doubt the efficacy of pure reductionism (as supplying a full and sufficient picture of the world) as foolish and wrong-headed—so claiming, it would seem, to have found in reductionism the secrets of the universe—he is elsewhere much more cautious and seems to doubt his own wild statements. In the preface of his book for instance he admits that not everything in chemistry can be predicted or resolved by quantum theory—which amounts to saying that it is not possible to effectively reduce chemistry to physics. Again he stresses the extreme improbability, perhaps the zero probability, of the emergence of life from inanimate matter. If he is right in this again he is denying the possibility of reductionism. Yet again he points out that the genetic code consists of at least fifty macro-molecular components which are themselves coded in DNA. It follows from this that the code cannot be translated except by using certain products of its translation. This constitutes, as he candidly admits, a really baffling circle. Again he seems to have no real conviction that it will ever be possible—and is perhaps logically impossible—to explain the mental in terms of the material. In fact I think it is not too much to say that the book has two quite distinct parts or strands, one written by a highly able and most professional molecular biologist. The other by a confused, emotional and amateur philosopher. Alternating with passages of marvellous cocksuredness we find statements of caution and relative humility. We also find in the section entitled "The Kingdom and the Darkness" dramatic rhetoric which reveals a passionate involvement in the tragedy of the human situation. Thus he says that science has the terrible capacity to destroy: not only bodies but the soul itself. But what can a complete reductionist mean by the word "soul"? He does not say!

The principle of the matter is, of course, that reductionism by itself does not provide any complete answers.

As Sir Karl Popper[2] has pointed out scientists have to be reductionists in the sense that nothing is as great a success in science as successful reduction. Indeed it is perhaps the most successful form conceivable of all scientific explanations since it results in the identification of the unknown with the known. Scientists have to be reductionists in their methods—either naïve or else more or less critical reductionists. But Sir Karl Popper also points out that hardly any major reduction in science has ever been completely successful. There is almost always an unresolved residue left by even the most successful attempts at reduction; and yet another point—Popper is of the convinced opinion that there are no reasons at all in favour of philosophical reductionism. But even after all this it is clear that working scientists must continue attempting reductions for the reason that we learn an immense amount from unsuccessful attempts at reduction and the problems left open in this way belong to the most valuable intellectual possessions of science. We can briefly sum up Popper's conclusions by saying that (1) we cannot reduce or hope to reduce biology to physics, or to physics and chemistry, (2) we cannot reduce to biology the subjective conscious experiences which we may ascribe to animals nor of course can we reduce these further to physics and chemistry, and (3) we cannot completely reduce

[2] Sir Karl Popper, (1974, in press) in Dobzhansky, T. and Ayala, F. (Eds.) *Chance and Creativity in Evolution.*

the consciousness of self and the creativeness of the human mind either to animal experience or *a fortiori* to physics and chemistry. So reductionists we as scientists must remain; but only in the sense that reductionism is a necessary part of our intellectual adventure. We need something more than this, we need as P. W. Anderson recently said *"some combination of inspiration, analysis and synthesis"*. Analysis is reductionist; but inspiration and synthesis are most certainly not. Above all we must not be mislead into adherence to any form of philosophical reductionism.

I think I have said enough to make it clear that the use and misuse of reduction is indeed one of the major methodological problems of science today. So it is immensely important that the issue be thoroughly debated from all aspects and there is no better springboard for such debate than that provided by Monod's book.

It is therefore most satisfactory that the editor has been able to gather such a varied and learned band of contributors together, none of whom is responsible for any views but his own. We thus have a varied spectrum of opinion not in any way committed to one position.

If I have any particular regret it is that it was unavoidably impossible to obtain a contribution from that towering representative of modern theoretical physics, Werner Heisenberg—for what an accession an essay from him would have been! However in a work published some years ago but only recently issued in English translation (*Physics and Beyond*, Allen & Unwin 1972), Heisenberg has expressed with simplicity and directness his conception of the "stable ground" which underlies both the scientific and religious experience of mankind, but which the philosophy of Monod lacks. Heisenberg there states it as his belief that the problem of values implies a compass by which man must steer his ship through life. This compass is none other than his relationship to "the central order"—the "one" with which we commune in the language of religion. This religion he says must win out. For the very idea of truth is involved with the reality of religious experiences. Western man's views of good and evil still do, and must always, reflect the ethical norm of Christianity. If this compass, depending as it does on the central order, should ever become extinguished the result would indeed be disastrous for mankind.

CHAPTER TWO

# *The Problem of Faith and Reason*

MARY WARNOCK

Jacques Monod is, professionally, a molecular biologist who shared the Nobel Prize in 1965 for his work on genetics. As an amateur, he is a philosopher. The book I am going to discuss contains a combination of his amateur and his professional interests. *Chance and Necessity* is a best seller in France, Germany and the United States: what I am mainly concerned with is why it has had such an overwhelming success.

Professor Monod argues that, through recent advances in molecular biology and genetics "the secret of life", so long sought after, has more or less been discovered, the fact in itself makes it imperative for the serious biologist, who holds this secret, to try to formulate the connections between his kind of thought (the forms of his thought, Professor Monod says) and thought in general: that is, the presuppositions of philosophers and of ordinary people who are not biologists. Biology of all the sciences, both because it is of such central interest to men, and because it has undergone such radical advances, has, as it were, a duty to mankind, and particularly a duty to philosophers, to relate its findings to thought as a whole. This is the overriding purpose of Professor Monod's book. The argument goes more or less as follows.

Life itself, the very existence of life, has been shown to be the result of chance mutations which could not have been predicted. Therefore, Monod argues, there can be no general purpose in the existence of life: no reason for it can be given, since it need not have existed. Therefore no system of religion or of ethics which presupposes such reason or purpose can be viable. This is the first negative conclusion of his argument. The positive conclusion, which seems to him to follow, is this: the only tenable attitude to the world is the objective attitude, which is, and always has been, the attitude of the scientist. By "objective" Monod means non-emotive and unprejudiced in favour of human affairs rather than other phenomena. To adopt the objective attitude is, in his use of the term, *ipso facto* to reject the concept of any intention or purpose in life and therefore to reject the possibility of religion. And so the negative and the affirmative parts of this initial statement amount to the same thing.

Up to now, Monod suggests, all systems of thought have been either vitalistic or animistic. And both kinds of system are completely incompatible with true objectivity, though both may accommodate the existence of necessity in nature, exemplified in the theory of evolution. Vitalist theories, of which Monod discusses that of Bergson, postulate an absolute gulf between living things and inanimate things, and hold that there is some purpose or direction in which living things, and they alone, develop. But Monod is more interested in what he describes as animism. Everyone except Bergson emerges as an animist. Animism is supposed to hold that a purpose is being worked out throughout the whole of the universe: in evolution, in history, or in some other way. Man has, it is true, a special place in the universe, but he is essentially part of it. Primitive peoples have always tried to bridge the apparent gap between the animate and inanimate by giving spirits to things. Marx and Teilhard de Chardin are guilty of animism in more subtle ways, though they are no less mistaken, in that they see the development of evolution or of history as tending towards a particular goal, everything in the world being as it were of one stuff and all working together for good. If one takes the notion of objectivity seriously and understands in the light of it the totally chance origin of life, which once it has arisen is then governed by necessity, then neither vitalism nor animism will do. The whole idea of purpose, whether for humans only or for the whole of nature, must be expurgated.

It was from the supposed connections between men and the world that philosophers have thought that they could deduce values. So if animism is dropped the message is, there is no longer any excuse for thinking that values can be deduced at all. Every philosopher up to the present is supposed to have been guilty of the naturalistic fallacy of trying to derive conclusions about how things ought be from an interpretation of how things are. But they were wrong about how things are, and they have lost their last excuse for committing the naturalistic fallacy. We are left, it is true, with the phenomenon of the human spirit, but we have no means of deducing from its nature, nor from the nature of things at large, any values whatsoever. What we can see is man at a certain stage of development, in which cultural and social evolution has gone along with and influenced physical evolution in such a way that man is now capable, if he so decides, of destroying himself without waiting for the forces of evolution to do it for him. Man is now capable of suicide, or rather of genocide. All the factors which make for success in modern life, factors such as intelligence and imagination, make for the success of the individual but not necessarily for the success of the human race as a whole. There are grave dangers, we are told, facing us genetically speaking, but here Monod is not referring to the over-population of the earth, nor to the pollution of our environment. He is referring, he says, to a sickness of the spirit. Throughout history there has been a continuous process of selection of ideas, and the ideas which have survived have been, tautologically enough, those that were fitted to survive: those which gave men confidence in their dealings with the world. Now far the most effective attitude to the world, and that which is most liable therefore to survive and to lead towards the survival of the race, is the scientific or objective attitude, which at this stage in the argument is reintroduced through a different entrance. And the moment has come, Monod tells us, when people must begin to accept it thoroughly. Such an attitude is already accepted as far as the discoveries and techniques of life go, but there is a refusal to accept objectivity with respect to its ethical and religious consequences. Men still insist upon pretending to a source of values which does not in fact exist. And the sickness which threatens mankind is in fact identical with this pretence. It is the lie in the soul. In the presuppositions of philosophers, theologians and ordinary people there is a contradiction. They believe in science, but will not accept its atheistical consequences. Now this deep lie produces fear, a fear which is often rationalised as having as its object some one or other of the creations of science itself (such as the bomb or chemical fertilisers), but which in fact is directed against science itself. It is quite simply a fear of facing the facts. It is now time, Monod says, for man to wake up out of his dream.

When he does wake up, he will recognise an absolute gulf between facts and values. He will never again commit the naturalistic fallacy. To commit it, to confuse knowledge with values, is to indulge in inauthentic thought. Authenticity, both in action and in discourse, consists in recognising the difference between them. However, it must be recognised, the argument goes on, that the rule "don't confuse facts with values" is itself a moral rule or discipline. It can't itself be derived from any state of affairs. Thus to decide to believe in objectivity, as we are urged to do, is to decide on a new system of ethics, to be called the ethics of knowledge. But in adopting such a system, we must recognise that we have chosen the system for ourselves. We have decided on obedience to the commandment—"no naturalism". It has not been imposed on us from without. So Monod is here urging a Kantian-style Copernican revolution according to which we come to understand that it is our own rule which creates the world of values. The values are not consequences of any absolute or independent rule. Only the adoption of this system of ethics can save us because, we are told, it is the only practical ethics. The disease we suffer from, the lie in the soul, is the result of a contradiction between scientific knowledge and old-style animistic ethics. Adopt the new-style ethics and we shall be cured. Men can survive provided that they adopt some goal beyond self-interest, and the ethics of knowledge provides them with such a goal. Ethics must therefore be freely founded on the scientific attitude and on nothing else. All other ethical values must be seen to be derived from the basic value which is understanding.[1] We must choose knowledge. Choosing this, the highest value, is choosing the kingdom of ideas, and rejecting the darkness of ignorance, deception and superstition.

It is impossible even to summarise Monod's argument without lapsing into a rhetorical mood if not into actual rhetoric: the last chapter of the book, with its clarion call to reason and understanding, its dark threats of ruin if any other choice is made, its deployment of emotive words like "authenticity" and "freedom", is presumably that which will have the greatest appeal. But of course the rhetoric would be far less effective if it did not come as a climax after a good deal of scientific talk. Ethical systems have always been most powerful and attractive when derived from something other than merely ethical considerations. So, the system of Spinoza depends for its appeal on the fact that it is a small part of a complete metaphysical description of the world and man's place in it. And Monod's ethical appeal is largely a result of the apparent deduction of his conclusions from the hard facts of molecular biology. But of course he is wary enough to see that, put

[1] In the Royal Institution discussion, Monod, challenged on this point, declared that many other choices will have to be made. These will be axiomatic and from them we must be able to construct a system of ethics compatible with the twentieth century. (Ed.)

like this, the whole thing looks like a monstrous example of the very crime he is inveighing against—namely, the naturalistic fallacy. So it suddenly and unexpectedly at the end turns out that he derives science from ethics rather than ethics from science. The ultimate choice of the scientific attitude, without which science itself would be impossible, is the free choice of man himself. It is not imposed from without. It need not be made, but it is the only hope of salvation.

There is no doubt that the French have a particular talent for this kind of thing. The most difficult and sensitive judgment has to be made in writing history or philosophy or literary criticism as to how general an argument can get, and still make sense and still be accepted. It is well known that an unqualified generalisation without evidence is boring and, even if it is true, its truth is not understood until some of the evidence which led up to it is produced. Merely to state that something or other is the case is not enough. It is necessary at least to appear to derive it from something else, something less general and more available than itself. It is here, it seems to me, that the peculiar talent of the French lies. They have a knack of picking on some familiar fact, or on some apparently unconnected phenomenon, or some scientific law, and using it in a manner that combines high mindedness with an element of surprise, to conjure up a conclusion as wide ranging as you like, yet having apparently, because of its humble origins, an awful connection with you and me, with the here and now. Thus Sartre is able to derive vast consequences about the nature of existence from the familiar fact that one feels ashamed if caught eavesdropping at a keyhole. Monod does not, it is true, deploy familiar facts but his facts are incontrovertible because they come from the mouth of so great an authority. He is able to argue that there is one, and only one, course of action that we must all take or perish, from the apparently disconnected phenomena of molecular biology. His facts are the more impressive as a source of all ethics since they will be perfectly unintelligible to most of his readers, but facts they must be, since they are presented in the smartest possible diagrams.

Besides the conjuring trick of producing the conclusions out of the premises, both Sartre and Monod have another best-selling feature in common. They both appear to bridge the gap between the cultures, or at least to break down the barriers between philosophy, literature and, in Monod's case, science as well. It is not clear whether this is more exciting for the scientists who may feel that they are now in a position to tell the philosophers about ethics, or for the literary who may feel that they have grasped the form of scientific thought, and can now dictate to the philosophers and the scientists alike. There will certainly be many readers in England who will enjoy this book above all because it will seem to prove that there is no need for different subjects to be kept different. Everyone can have a go at everything. For Monod is the new Teilhard de Chardin—atheistical, it is true, but with an urgent message and precise instructions for us all—and he will appeal, I think, to those who look always for a secret, a solution, an answer to everything.

But there remain with me two or three pedantic but obstinate doubts. First of all, I am not sure that the conclusions actually follow from the premises. Monod admits ignorance of the absolute origins of the systems he examines. Might it not be that some creative god made a system which could by chance throw up any kind of thing, living or lifeless? It is not necessarily the case that this creative god would be without interest in whatever was in this sense thrown up by the chance of the mutations. If someone wished to provide a theistic answer to the question how it all started I see no reason why he should not, nor would the god so supposed necessarily be indifferent to the conduct of the creatures even if, to start off with, there had been no precise plan for them in the creator's mind. Second, it does not seem to me enough merely to *state* that all systems of morality hitherto invented were guilty of the naturalistic fallacy. There have been many philosophers who, rightly or wrongly, have gone to great lengths to identify and to avoid this fallacy. The theory that morality cannot be founded on natural facts is not new. It is not therefore clear that when men wake up out of their dogmatic slumber they will be quite so astonished as Monod would have us believe to find themselves without naturalistic foundations to their ethical beliefs. Lastly, we are told that we must at all costs adopt the ethics of knowledge which is identical with choosing to regard scientific knowledge as the highest value. But what exactly *is* the ethics of knowledge? What is the kingdom that we are to choose in preference to the darkness? The difficulty with rhetoric is that you may read it late at night and think that you have the secret of life, but you may wake up in the morning as sometimes out of a dream, and find that the secret, or at least its meaning, has escaped you.

## CHAPTER THREE

# *Chance, Potentiality and God*

ARTHUR PEACOCKE

If this were to be a sermon which I was to contribute to a new volume of holy writ, of which Professor Monod was to be the chief apostle, then I could do no better than take as my text, words from the book of the Lord Russell, both for their realism and their haunting beauty: "That Man is the product of causes which had no prevision of the end they were achieving; that his origin, his growth, his hopes and fears, his loves and beliefs, are but the outcome of accidental collocations of atoms; . . . all these things, if not quite beyond dispute, are yet so nearly certain that no philosophy which rejects them can hope to stand. Only within the scaffolding of these truths, only on the firm foundation of unyielding despair, can the soul's habitation henceforth be safely built."[1] For this passage, written in the 1920s, represents the abyss into which both Russell and Monod peer and the noble courage with which they respond to it, as they both "whistle in the dark". Although Monod writes from the vantage point afforded by the pinnacle of modern molecular biology, I believe the dark prospect he perceives has long been apparent to earlier generations in the Anglo-Saxon world—for example, Tennyson's *In Memoriam* reveals an anguish at the severance between the moral and material world quite as acute as that of Russell, some eighty years later. Be that as it may, the principal keystone of Monod's work raises in this Anglo-Saxon reader a reaction somewhat *déjà vu*. This keystone is, as readers of this volume are now well aware, the contrast between the "chance" processes which bring about mutations in the genetic material of an organism and the "necessity" of their consequences in the well-ordered, replicative, interlocking mechanism

[1] *Mysticism and Logic, and other Essays*, London, Edward Arnold, pp. 47–8.

which constitutes that organism's continuity as a living form. More specifically, mutations in DNA are the results of chemical or physical events and their location in the genome are entirely random with respect to the biological needs of the organism. Those that are incorporated into the genome of the organism (i.e., if they are not lethal) are only permanently so incorporated if, in interacting with its environment, the differential reproduction rate of the mutated form is advantageous. So put, and I think I have been fair to Monod, this is already something of a gloss on neo-Darwinism orthodoxy—as I shall have cause to mention later. But, even if we take it as it stands, it cannot be said to add anything very new *in principle* to the debates of the last 100 years. For the essential crux in these debates was, and is, that the mechanism of variation was causally entirely independent of the processes of selection, so that (as I have said) mutations were regarded as purely random with respect to the selective needs of the organism—and were so regarded long before the molecular mechanism of transmission, and alteration, of genetic information was unravelled in the last two decades. However that mechanism *has* now been elucidated and Monod describes it beautifully and clearly in its setting in the total functioning of living organisms.

The general conclusion he draws is, not surprisingly, like that of Russell in that he sees man, and so all the works of his mind and culture, as the products of pure chance and therefore without any cosmic significance. The universe must be seen not as a cosmos, that is a directionally ordered whole, but as a giant Monte Carlo saloon in which the dice have happened to fall out in the way which produced man. There is, according to Monod, no general purpose in the universe and in the existence of life (and so none in the universe as a whole). It need not, it might not, have existed—nor might man. Therefore any system of philosophy or religion which presupposes any plan or intention in the universe is founded on a fallacy, now fully exposed by the molecular-biological account of DNA and its mutations. The only attitude which is adoptable in the face of this is one of "objectivity", as he calls it—which he regards as non-emotive and not prejudiced in favour of man over other natural phenomena. The adoption of this "principle of objectivity" puts out of court all systems of thought which try to show that there is any sort of harmony between man and the universe and that man is a predictable, if not indispensable, product of the evolution of the universe. Those systems of thought, which this "principle of objectivity" of Monod rejects, include, of course, "vitalism" (said to be represented in its "metaphysical" form by Bergson and in its "scientific" form by Elsässer and Polanyi) and all forms of cosmic "animism", which sees a purpose being worked out in at least some aspect of the universe. This spurned "animism" is a remarkable collection for it includes dialectical materialism (notably the ideas of Engels, who draws most of Monod's fire), Judeo-Christianity (especially in any Teilhardian form), and a large part of Western philosophy. All exponents of these, he says, have constructed *a posteriori* ideological edifices designed to justify preconceived ethico-political theories. Needless to say the philosophers[2] have descended upon Monod in all their wrath—not without some wry smiles from the various kinds of Christian spectators of the game left at the turnstiles! It is not surprising that the philosophers are also scornful of those sections of the book where he imputes the naturalistic fallacy (that of trying to derive "ought" statements from "is" statements) to all "animist" philosophers, which in his language means all philosophers except those who now adopt his "principal of objectivity"—for what "is", according to Monod, is the product of chance and indifferent to man and his aspirations. But, what is interesting to me and what is nobly expressed in his own special style, is that Monod is deeply concerned for man's future and also that he recognises man as a unique product of evolution, with his brain and ability to communicate by language; and he urges, with great force, that man must choose a system of values, since man as an individual person and as a society, has to live, and to live means to act, and to act is to choose (shades of Sartre). The system of values which he espouses is based on his "ethic of knowledge", which is set in a mould of ideas distinctly existentialist, and he has, on both counts, been criticised by professional philosophers on this side of the Channel.

Nevertheless when the philosophers have had their say, the chief attraction of Monod's book to those of a scientific temper of mind is that it starts from the most accurate view of the physical and biological world available to us—namely, that afforded by natural science—and tries to understand man's significance in the world thus perceived. This seems to me to be an absolutely necessary exercise and let none of my criticisms, already given or those to come, of Monod's position be allowed to diminish at all my applaud at the attempt—

[2] Cf., Stephen Toulmin, "*French Toast*", New York Review of Books, Dec. 16, 1971, p. 17ff. and Stuart Hampshire, "*Molecular Philosophy*", *Observer Review*, May 7, 1972.

especially as I am now about to launch my own ship from the same home-port. I will in the end find myself navigating towards a different destination, but at least I recognise Monod as a fellow-voyager on these rough and dangerous seas. I now turn to an account of the particular course I prefer to steer in these troubled waters by looking again at

*The Scientific perspective on matter and man.*

In the last 100 years the perspective of the sciences concerned with the origin and development of the physical and biological worlds has, or should have, altered our attitude to the natural surroundings which human minds appear to transcend as subjects. For our familiar environment of stone, water, air, earth, grass, birds, animals and so on, are seen in this perspective no longer to be a kind of stage for the enactment of the human drama but to share with man common molecular structures and to be stages in a common continuous development in time.

Although this continuity of man with the organic world had sometimes been accepted in principle,[3] it was only just over 100 years ago that the scientific evidence for man's relation to other species began to appear and it is only in the last few decades that the emergence of primitive living organisms from inorganic matter could be outlined in any fashion which had a scientific basis in the new knowledge of biological evolution and of molecular biology and in new insights into the development of the physical cosmos.

The broad picture is familiar enough: how the nuclei of atoms more complex than hydrogen (which is the simplest atom and appears to be the basic material of the universe, for it occurs everywhere) are held together; how these atoms can combine to form molecules of a complexity increasing from the diatomic $H_2$ molecules up to those large molecules, containing tens of thousands of atoms, which constitute the enzymes and genetical material (DNA) of living organisms; how these macro-molecules interlock structurally and functionally with small molecules in an aqueous matrix so as to have the characteristics of living matter in cells; how living organisms, containing such cells, have developed in time on the surface of the planet Earth, itself the outcome of vast processes in immense conglomerations of matter on an astronomical scale.

However, there is one stage in this development on which I

[3] e.g., Genesis ii. 7: "And the Lord God formed man out of the dust of the ground and breathed into his nostrils the breath of life."

wish to re-focus, since it occupies a key position in Monod's thesis—namely the randomness of the molecular events on which natural selection is based. The whole context of the fundamental idea of natural selection of living organisms has been amplified, since Darwin and Wallace, by our knowledge of the existence of genetic factors, "genes", located in cell nuclei and constituted by molecules of DNA. This DNA, whose molecular patterns *are* the genes, are subject, as already mentioned, to sudden changes ("mutations") as a result of irradiation or chemical events and these molecular changes are random with respect to the biological needs of the organisms. It is this which so impresses Monod that he regards all living forms, including man, as the products of "chance". For the processes of natural selection (which are now increasingly seen to be much more subtle than previously thought, involving a complex interplay of heredity, environment, mutation and behaviour) that favour the survival of particular mutated organisms can only operate among the spectrum of possibilities provided by the random chemical events at the level of the DNA. Unlike Monod, I see no reason why this randomness of molecular event in relation to biological consequence has to be raised to the level almost of a metaphysical principle in interpreting the cosmos. For in the behaviour of matter on a larger scale, many regularities, which have been raised to the peerage of "laws", arise from the combined effects of random microscopic events which constitute the macroscopic (e.g., Boyle's Law and its dependence on molecular kinetics and all of statistical thermodynamics). It would be more accurate to say that the full gamut of possible forms of living matter could only be explored through the agency of the rapid and frequent randomisation which is possible at the molecular level of the DNA. This view leads to a quite different interpretation from that of Monod. After all, the random molecular events in DNA have occurred in a system which has the properties it has because its constituent atoms and molecules have *their* characteristic properties. In other words, the emergence of the immense variety of living forms manifests the potentialities of matter. That it does so through an exploration of all available possibilities by random molecular events does not seem to me to be in itself a sufficient basis for any apotheosis of "chance". Thus biological evolution no more qualifies for description as a "chance" process than any other. There is, nevertheless, a particularity about biological evolution since, once a variation has been favoured in an organism in a habitat in a particular location, the future variations which will then be favourable to that organism will be the result of the interplay of these variations past and present with the climatic and other factors (including other creatures) in its particular environment. The imprinting of the new variation yields gains in viability at the expense of channelling and limiting future possibilities. Because of this channelling effect of contingent circumstances it is quite likely the case that *all* possible modes of organisation of matter have not yet been elicited even by this random running through of the available possibilities, so that one cannot exclude the possibility of other forms of matter, both living and non-living, occurring in other parts of the universe. However, all observations suggest that the component parts of these hypothetical structures will obey the laws we have been able to observe on and from the Earth. Moreover, the existence of this hypothetical possibility need not detract us from considering the significance of the manifestation of those potentialities of matter that we have been able to observe on the Earth and notably in its biosphere. It is worth recalling some of the features of this cosmic development or "evolution" (in the strict, O.E.D., sense of "an appearance (of events, etc.) in due succession").

The whole of the present variety of living organisms, and of all of those species long since extinct, can be tracked back in a continuous line to those one, or a few, ordered aggregates of molecules which first acquired the ability to replicate themselves and grow by incorporating surrounding molecules. A "materialistic" view of our existence and of that of all living organisms is apparently justified, if linked with an important qualification which is that we recognise that the most significant of the "properties of matter" is that, organised in certain ways, it has the characteristics we call living and, indeed, human too. The primordial nebular cloud of hydrogen—or of its subnuclear "particulate" predecessors—has developed into living organisms and into man, with all his special qualities, achievements and potentialities for sublimity and degradation. *If* we are prepared to recognise that matter, the stuff of the universe, has this character and that the continuity I have described is from hydrogen atoms to the personalities and creative genius of men at their most developed, then it would still be legitimate to call the process "materialistic".

Each transition (e.g., the origin of life) within the cosmic development can be seen, in the light of our present-day scientific knowledge, to proceed in accordance with regularities in parallel observations we can make in or infer from our present experimental and theoretical investigation of the world we know. Briefly, we can say the cosmic development has proceeded by natural "law", using this term simply to denote the ordered and regular character of the knowledge which scientific investigation yields by the methodologies it has established. It is important to stress that the cosmic development presents us with an ordered behaviour of matter which is not abrogated, so it seems to me, by its depending on the random, chance character of the micro-events which underlie the regularities of many kinds of macro-observation (e.g., the naturally selected phenotypic changes following on a random chemical modification of DNA or Boyle's Law on the random collisions of gas molecules).

The cosmic development is, moreover, apparently a process in which new forms of organisation of matter emerge. The description of evolution as displaying "emergence" is often also used to point to the difficulty of fully explaining the mode of being of the newly appearing form in terms of its immediate, and certainly of its distant, predecessors. It is important to realise that it is reasonable to affirm and recognise this emergent character of the cosmic development, as for example Polanyi[4] does, without thereby intending to postulate in any sense any special super-added force or principle ("élan vital", "entelechy", "life force") which somehow mysteriously distinguishes living organisms from their non-living components. For the principle applies equally (as Polanyi rightly argues, it seems to me) to the logical (not contingent) impossibility of reducing the principles of operation of, for example, a steam engine to the physics and chemistry of each of its components considered separately.

New properties, functions and abilities have genuinely emerged in the successive stages of the cosmic development and this may now be taken as a datum of our thinking. The laws, principles and categories of thinking and vocabulary needed to describe each stage of this process will be particular to and characteristic of it. In this sense, chemistry is not "nothing-but" physics, especially not the physics of the nucleus; nor is biology "nothing-but" physics and chemistry; nor is human psychology and sociology "nothing-but" biology. All these ascriptions, which aspire to subsume the more developed form in terms of the intellectual concepts and experimental approaches which have succeeded at the lower and especially the immediately preceding levels,

[4] Polanyi, *Personal Knowledge*, London, Routledge and Kegan Paul, 1958.

constitute, in my view, a mistaken analysis of the modes of investigation which each level of organisation of matter renders necessary for its understanding.

Even allowing for our natural anthropomorphism there are nevertheless good grounds for emphasising that man represents a point of biological development in which many tendencies have reached a pre-eminently high level, e.g., ability to expand into new environments, adaptability, complexity of structure and behaviour, protected reproduction and care of the young, awareness of and flexible reaction to the environment, socialisation, individualisation and communication by language. These are purely biological criteria and if we are to interpret the whole cosmic development honestly then we are bound to look at all the facts. Yet a full description of the man who has emerged in the universe goes beyond his purely biological features, even if these are as highly developed as those just listed (but let us note that man's linguistic ability is now widely regarded as so separated from that of the highest primate as to be unique). One's assessment of the nature of man has a determinative influence at this point. Thus the challenge of the presence of man in the universe as the outcome of evolution evokes various responses among scientists. To Monod it is a stark fact but in itself not significant as regards the nature of the cosmos, for he regards man as the consequence of mere "chance" events at the molecular level of the DNA of his living progenitors and bases his view of man's significance on a particular interpretation of and emphasis on this role of "chance". But to other scientists it is a false modesty, verging on intellectual perversity "to renounce, in the name of scientific objectivity, our position as the highest form of life on earth and our own advent by a process of evolution as the most important problem *of* evolution", as Polanyi affirms[5]—in concurrence with Eccles, Hinshelwood, Dobzhansky, Hardy, Thorpe.

For to take seriously, as scientists *qua* scientists ought, the presence of man as the outcome of the cosmic evolution of matter is to open up many questions which go far beyond the applicable range of languages, concepts and modes of investigation developed by the natural sciences for describing and examining the less developed and less complex forms of matter which preceded the emergence of man. For if the stuff of the world, the primeval concourse of hydrogen atoms or sub-nuclear particles, has as a matter of fact and not conjecture become man—man who possesses not only a social life and biological organisa-

[5] M. Polanyi, *The Tacit Dimension*, p. 47 London, Routledge and Kegan Paul 1967.

tion but also an "inner", self-conscious life in relation to others, which make him personal—then how *are* we properly to speak of the cosmic development if after aeons of time the atoms have become human beings, persons? Moreover, paradoxically and significantly, knowledge of the process by which they have arrived in the world seems to be confined to human beings. We alone reflect on our atomic and simpler forbears and we alone adjust our behaviour in the light of this perspective. To ignore the glory, the predicament and the possibilities of man in assessing the trend and meaning of the cosmic development would be as unscientific as the former pre-Copernican account of the universe, based as it was on the contrary prejudice. Apparently, by a continuous development under the control of the regular processes of natural laws, new forms of matter have creatively emerged out of the nuclear particles and atoms of several thousand million years ago and have now in man become conscious of themselves. From man's consciousness new creativities of a specifically human kind have erupted, notably in men of genius but, just as significantly, also in the very real individual creativity of each human being within his own social environment a creativity which, however humble, far transcends that of the highest animal.

Thus the perspective of science on the world raises acutely certain questions which by their very nature cannot be answered from within the realm of discourse of science alone.

1. What sort of cosmos is it if the original primeval mass of hydrogen atoms has (maybe by pure randomness, which is just the surest way of trying out all the possible permutations and combinations) eventually manifested the potentiality of becoming organised in material forms such as ourselves which are conscious and even *self*-conscious, can reflect, and love and hate, and pray, have ideas, can discourse with each other, can exhibit the creative genius of a Mozart or Shakespeare, or display the personal qualities of a Socrates or Jesus of Nazareth?

2. How can we explain the existence of such a cosmos of *this* particular character, outlined above? It seems to me that any explanation (not cause in the cause-effect sequence of our space-time) of the existence of such a cosmos to be plausibly adequate must be one that grounds this existence in a mode of being which is other than the cosmos so described and which transcends mental activity as much as mental activity transcends physical processes. Such a cosmos-explaining-

entity must be *not less* than personal or mental in its nature. Its (?his) existence would make it more comprehensible how matter could possess the potentiality of the mental activity evidenced in man than would the designation of "chance" alone (à la Monod) as a sufficient explanation of the cosmos. The role of randomness in natural processes does not of itself preclude the possibility of the existence of such an entity which, as Aquinas would say, "men call God". So we come explicitly to the question of

*God and the cosmos.*

To the Christian theologian, the question of God is prior to the question of man and matter. The essentially new element which the scientific perspective inevitably introduces into the theistic concept of creation in its classical form is the realisation that the cosmos which is sustained and held in being by God (this sustaining and holding itself constituting "creation") is a cosmos which has always been in process of producing new emergent forms of matter. It is a world which is still being made and, on the surface of the Earth at least, man has emerged from biological life and his history is still developing. Any static conception of the way in which God sustains and holds the cosmos in being is therefore precluded, for the cosmos is in a dynamic state and, in the corner which we as men can observe, has evolved conscious and self-conscious minds who shape their environment and choose between ends.

That the world was in a flux and change, with all its corollaries for the destiny of the individual man, has been reflected upon since the ancient Greeks. But that the matter of the world developed in a particular direction to more complex, and ultimately thinking, forms was not established knowledge. The people of Israel, and following them, the Christian Church, have traditionally believed in the providential hand of God in human history, with the non-human world being regarded simply as the stage for that drama. Science now sees man as part of "nature" and both together as subject to continuous development. If the emergence of new forms of matter in the world is in some way an activity of God, then this creative action must be regarded as his perennial activity and not something already completed and entirely in the past. The scientific perspective of a cosmos in development introduces a dynamic element into our understanding of God's relation to the cosmos which was previously obscured, although never excluded.

The convergence of the lines of thought which see God (usually designated, in this context as "Holy Spirit") as immanent in the cosmos in general, in man in particular, and as consummated in Jesus and in the community expressing his spirit, is, I would suggest, peculiarly consonant with the scientific perspective. For in that scientific perspective we see a cosmos in which creativity is ever-present, in which new forms of matter emerge and in which, with many fruitless directions, nevertheless in the end there emerged man, mind, human society, human values, in brief what people call the "human spirit". These two perspectives from, on the one hand, the Hebrew and Christian experience and, on the other, the gamut of the sciences, mutually illuminate each other. Each has its own autonomy and justification but, if both are recognised, a combined insight into the cosmic development is then afforded in which, it seems to me, the features elaborated by the sciences are in harmony with the experiences which cluster around particular events in history and which theological language expounds. The Christian theological interpretation complements and develops the scientific account in the significance it attributes to these events in human history. Moreover the theological perspective, if accepted, gives meaning to the present, and a sense of direction for the future to a world still regarded as in process and as the matrix of new emergent forms of human life.

The theological perspective itself is correspondingly reshaped by this consideration of the scientific account of the cosmic development. For the theological account will now be seen to be most meaningful and to correspond best with the scientific one, when it emphasises that God is immanent, that his action in the world is continuously creative, and that the coming of Christ and the role of the Church are to be understood in such dynamic terms, rather than in the more classical and static images of earlier theological exposition. The two perspectives are complementary, for the scientific provides the necessary grounding in material reality which the theological requires, and the theological provides the means whereby contemporary man in his community can consciously participate and find both personal and corporate meaning in a cosmic process which, without the Christian perspective, would appear impersonal and even inimical. The first Christians found themselves inevitably using language which was an extension of that applied to persons and so corresponded to the highest they knew, about that power of God (as "Holy Spirit"), which through

Jesus had possessed them. In accordance with this, and indeed, as a kind of extension of it, the Christian understanding is that the meaning of the cosmic process revealed by science is ultimately to be expressed in personal terms in the sense that the language of human personality is the least misleading for describing the direction in which the process moves.

However, the contemporary Christian theist in stressing the immanent creativity of God in the cosmos must recognise that it is by the "laws" and through the regularities of nature that God must be presumed to be working. This recognition is linked with the important understanding that matter is of such a kind and the "laws" which it obeys are of such a kind, that creativity, in the sense of the emergence of new forms of matter, is a permanent potentiality whose actualisation depends on circumstances. This potentiality is not injected into the cosmos from "outside" either by God, or by a Life Force, élan vital, or other supposedly "supernatural" agency. If God is in the world-process of matter at all, he is in it all through, in all its potentialities, whether actualised or not, and he continues to hold it in being by his will with these potentialities and not otherwise. It has long been recognised, and emphasised especially by the late C. A. Coulson, that to postulate a "God of the gaps" who is supposed to intervene to bridge the gap between, for example, the living and non-living is not only a tactical error on the part of theists (for science has a habit of bridging these gaps from its own resources!) but is to mistake entirely the relation between God and the cosmos. For, with hindsight, it seems almost an impertinence of men not to allow God to be creative in his own way through the stuff of the cosmos and its regular mutual interrelationships, or the "laws" it obeys, and to assert that he had both brought matter into existence and had to intervene from time to time to help it on to the next stage which he, presumably, willed—the transition from non-living to living, or the special creation of individual species, notably man himself, or the creation of each individual human "soul". It now seems more consistent to urge that God has been creating all the time through eliciting all the possibilities of the matter which he had brought into existence endowed with certain potentialities and governed by the laws of its transformations; and that this exploration of potentialities rests on the statistical coverage available to random events at the micro level.

Hence Christians have no interest in finding evidence for any form of vitalism, as they and their critics have frequently supposed. To postulate a "special creation" of species or that God injected "life" into the universe or that God somehow directly and personally directs the processes of biological evolution by means other than that inherent in the nature of matter and its "laws" are all errors on *Christian* premises. The old theistic "argument from design", in spite of its evocative power, foundered on its inability by itself to show that the concept of an omnipotent architect and designer generated by reflection on the natural order actually had an object; and it was later vulnerable to the further criticism, based on biology, that what appeared to be the result of design, and so of the intention of a designer, in the biological world could, in principle at least if not always in detail, be more readily explained in terms of the operation of natural selection. Now, however, the sciences afforded a wider perspective and a sequence which itself can evoke, like religious language, a situation to which we respond by commitment and which, in its oddity, points to the appropriate logical status for the word "God", thus: baryons, nucleons, atoms, molecules, inorganic matter, nucleo-proteins, living matter, cells, cellular assemblies, fishes, mammals, conscious organisms, primates, *Homo sapiens*, Stone Age men, the inventor of fire, the inventor of the wheel, intelligent, self-conscious persons—and so on, and so on, taking many different lines of human excellence until the sequence evokes a disclosure and a commitment to values, "the light dawns", "the ice breaks", as the late Ian Ramsey characteristically used to say.[6]

Earlier, I suggested that Monod and I were at least fellow-voyagers setting out from the same home-port of the scientific perspective on the world. The course I have steered approaches a very different land-fall from that of Monod, and there are many features of the coast I would like to have pointed out, had I had space. I am not pretending that the journey by the route I have indicated will be any less stormy, indeed some nights may be darker, but, if we had time to travel this route further, I would suggest that a gleam of light could be discerned on the horizon, perhaps even that "day spring from on high" which was promised us. Either way, his or mine, our duty is clear—it is that first enjoined on self-conscious thinking man by Plato through the mouth of Socrates: "Our duty is to take whatever doctrine is best and hardest to disprove and embarking upon it as upon a craft, to sail upon it through life in the midst of dangers."

[6] I. T. Ramsey, *Religious Language*, London, 1957, e.g. p. 67.

CHAPTER FOUR

# *The Cartesian Paradox*

JOHN LEWIS

## *Part I: Two Worlds or One*

### *Beyond Descartes*

It would be a complete mistake to characterise Professor Monod as simply a reductionist, a materialist of the old school, content to see the whole of existence in terms of molecular physics. He understands much better than most of his readers and the general run of reductionist thinkers just what he is reducing and therefore eliminating. Indeed even while taking the final step, he pauses. He finds that he *cannot* reject the unique properties and behaviour of living organisms, still less of man. As a result at the same time, he *asserts* and he *denies*; and thus finds himself on the horns of a dilemma.

He would be indignant if we said that he is far more akin to the spirit of Teilhard in his awe, his humble recognition, of the miracle of living things. "Living creatures are strange objects", and yet in their qualitative uniqueness they have appeared "not by transgressing physical laws, but by exploiting them". Evolved by chance and by purely natural means, nevertheless they are controlled by the plan of their own complex systems of self-maintenance, and pursue inflexibly their own inner purpose and goal directed course.

> Objectivity obliges us to recognize the teleonomic character of living organisms, to admit that in their structure and performance they decide on and pursue a purpose.[1]

But purpose had no hand in their evolving.

[1] Monod, *Chance and Necessity*, Collins, London, 1972, p. 31.

His recognition of this, and of the still more significant appearance of mind, points forward to man's rational control of the world in terms of human needs and aspirations, and sees life in terms of its culmination here. His regretful but determined scientific objectivity sees all this as a mere lucky throw of the dice, as the highly improbable consequence of the blind interaction of physical units, with no pre-vision, no innate purposive striving, and no least care for the result, and the phenomena of life itself as no more than what fully explains it, physico-chemistry, and mind as ultimately the chemistry of the cortical neurones—no, the *physics* to which chemistry is reduced. Scientific objectivity compels this conclusion, however reluctant we are to accept it, however much it contradicts the facts of life and mind that equally compel our acceptance and our reverence.

Let us sharpen this paradox as Monod himself is anxious that we should. On the one side we see that all the functions of the body are based purely on the laws of physics and chemistry; all the activities of man can be found to be no more than an immense elaboration of blind physico chemical phenomena. Living beings are but minute and special cases of that vast and continuous redistribution of matter and energy which the physicist sees as the ultimate nature of the world and everything in it. And yet we *really* have, in Monod's own words, "a new kingdom: that of culture, of ideas, of knowledge".

### *The Uniqueness of Life*

It can hardly seem to many much more than an academic exercise whether a *chemical* formula retains its autonomy or is transformed into physical terms. Nearly all the discussions on scientific method are carried out by physicists, mathematicians and logicians, who often write as though they had never seen a living cell under the electron microscope. As we see it in a diagram or photograph, we think of it structurally, when we see it alive it is visibly a scene of furious purposive activity. The mitochondria are not static lumps but highly mobile, squirming worm-like back and forth across the cell spaces to where energy is needed. Everywhere there is movement, flow, change. This is a single cell; the structure of paramecium or vorticella is also monocellular, and still more diversified into functional organelles, still more vigorously engaged in perpetual movement, internal and external. Molecular biologists speak as if they had never watched a living animal in the wild: a squirrel, for instance. "There is so much suppleness, such unexpectedness, such exuberance of life and curiosity. . . . It takes interest, it flutters, it plays. Around it an aura of freedom begins to float, a glimmer of personality," as a distinguished man of science writes whose name might seriously upset Professor Monod if it were revealed.

And so for all its connection with and dependence on the inorganic, the realm of life exhibits a character unique, distinctive and qualitatively new. Each organism has an individuality which it is equipped to safeguard and maintain in a physical universe which everywhere else is levelling down and dissipating the ordered and varied to disorder and uniformity. Within limits it regenerates itself when injured, as a broken machine does not, restores wastage of tissue, reproduces others of the same unimaginable and unique complexity. In maintaining its own existence its resourcefulness ranges from successful adaptation, itself astounding, to active control.

Consider the living plant or animal. It takes in simple materials from its environment and synthesises them into complex carbon and nitrogenous compounds of extraordinary complexity and amazing functions like haemoglobin or adenosine triphosphate (ATP) or the chloroplasts in the cells of leaves. The bewildering range and multifarious functions of the constituent cells and cell products is related of course to the function of a complex whole, the organism itself. It feeds and synthesises. It also respires; it provides itself with an endless stream of energy both for motion and for its endothermic vital processes. We used to think this to be a simple oxidation process of the pattern of burning paper. We now know that it is an incredibly complex process known as the Krebs' cycle, controlled by a multitude of enzymes each effecting one link in the complex chain of chemical changes. This process, and also the equally complex process of photosynthesis, proceeds according to its own rules with perfect regularity and dependability, and nothing like it is known in the inanimate world.

Finally, unlike all the processes of the physical world, instead of entropy increasing it is decreasing. That is to say instead of the whole process running down, temperature equalising, disorder increasing, the organic processes are increasing their energy stores, increasing their orderliness and, in the mammal, raising its body temperature far above that of the environment. Life resists entropy. Its energy content remains stable or increases. This it does at the expense of the environment, drawing the opposite of entropy from it, or, to put it otherwise, freeing itself from the entropy it is creating by living.

It must not be imagined that Monod regards this unique behaviour of living organisms as an animistic and anthropocentric picture of which he profoundly disapproves. The paradox of his position is that he does see this as the culmination of the evolutionary process: a category of unique organic entities that having once appeared are unlikely ever to appear again.

Nor is Monod any less deeply impressed by the transition to man as a thinking being—a critical transformation, a mutation from zero to everything. Once again there are the necessary preconditions: the skeletal changes leading to the upright stance and the free arms and hands—the gradual, delicate, but highly successful modifications of ankle bones, wrist and fingers, to make walking possible and to give both the power and precision grip of the toolmaker; and the parallel and the corresponding modification of the skull and cranium to allow for the expansion of the brain and thus make possible an increase in intelligence. This in turn leads to the discovery of the tool. Thereafter by the selection of every chance brain improvement, on account of the advantage it gives to the tool user, we reach at last the power of speech and conceptual thought, making possible the modification and control of the environment. This immense step forward has been well described as "This sudden deluge of cerebralisation, this biological invasion of a new animal type, this irresistible tide of fields and factories, this immense and growing edifice of matter and ideas—a change of planetary magnitude."

*Man and Evolution*

It is argued that because man is an animal, a primate, and so on, he is *nothing but* an animal, or nothing but an ape with a few extra tricks. But this is to deny that he has *essential* attributes other than those of all other animals. Man is indeed an entirely new kind of animal in ways altogether fundamental for understanding him, and these are precisely the characteristic that are not shared with any other animal. In *Homo sapiens* we see the intelligence linked indissolubly with the habile hand, the upright stance, the power of speech and complex co-operative social work and organisation that reflects creatures not adapting to their environment but adapting and radically altering their environment to suit themselves, ultimately making a new environment and a civilisation.

And thus man breaks from his ancestry initiating a new form

of evolution, not genetic—incredibly slow, but technological and ideological—incredibly rapid. This has been described as a new form of heredity, the inheritance of learning through tradition and education:

> "The new evolution peculiar to man operates directly by the inheritance of acquired characters, of knowledge and learned activities which arise in and are continuously a part of an organismic environmental system, that of social organisation. In the new evolution we can inherit directly from ancestors dead two thousand years, or from our contemporaries half the world away from us."[2]

Thus the human species has properties unique to itself, appearing as the product of a creature not possessing such qualities. Purpose and plan were not in the process which produced them but purposes and plans are the essential character of the new stage of evolution.

What has thus appeared cannot be translated without remainder into the language of physics and chemistry, any more than the arguments of Monod's *Chance and Necessity*: they have a dimension of their own which cannot be described in purely molecular terms.

*Eliminating Life and Mind?*

Monod feels that it is necessary both to pay the fullest and most ungrudging tribute to life and to man: two remarkable phenomena—the gap between animate and inanimate only less incredible than that between animal and man. But at the same time he insists, rightly, as all of us contributing to this symposium would too, on this having taken place with no intervention in the operation of natural law. But he is compelled to go farther and fare worse. The thinking man presents an *appearance* which might suggest that physical law is transcended or supplemented. It is not. Each novelty, each unique process, is capable of ultimate analysis without remainder "to simple, obvious, mechanical interactions" and to the laws governing the behaviour of its least parts—its ultimate molecular constituents. Monod denies that on these higher levels new principles, new laws appear, even if it is the case that they do not derive from some supernatural source, but are the *function* of more highly organised matter as the organicists believe.

[2] George Gaylord Simpson, *The Meaning of Evolution.*

Monod is strongly critical of Polanyi and his fellow contributors to the symposium *Beyond Reductionism*,[3] all of whom, though they reject vitalism in every form and stand for a completely naturalistic account of the rising stages of evolutionary development, nevertheless assert the distinct qualitatively new properties of life as irreducible to, though dependent upon, physical interactions.

This Monod sees as Hegelian, that is to say, explained by an inner unfolding principle of reason, and condemns as the type of vitalist thinking "which, phoenix-like, is reborn in every generation".

It is important to understand just why Monod continuously asserts and as firmly denies the reality and objectivity of these new levels. He accepts them because he is an objective thinker, he denies them because he is a Cartesian metaphysician. Scientifically he can, of course, say that all the phenomena have their own, special, and necessary physical component on which the new qualities are dependent. No one denies this; but what is *necessary* to account for life, or for thought, is not *sufficient* to account for it because it leaves out the inescapable realities of life and thought themselves, and their unique processes, behaviour and principles. Monod argues as if the discovery that sound depends on vibrations of certain wavelengths, which are necessary of course, eliminates the sound as subjective sensation of a unique character, reducing it to physical movements. This, of course, also eliminates the complex and objective laws of harmony, the richness and significance of music itself. But are the grooves on the record, are the sound waves vibrating at a certain rate, more real than the music you hear? If the sonata *is* a musical composition then its reality is indubitable and final. That it *depends* on such vibrations does not diminish that reality but only indicates that complex realities of this kind are made up of different levels of reality.[4] Are we really to abolish sound, colour, all the richness of our cultural life by a complete reduction, in Monod's words of "*everything* to simple, obvious, mechanical interactions"?

But Monod is a Cartesian. Descartes argues, that the physical world exists quite independently of life and mind, and has only the properties of extension and motion. He justifies this as "a clear and distinct" idea that it is impossible to deny; and he shows further that

[3] (Eds. Koestler and Smythies, 1969.) A similar position to that of Polanyi is taken by Needham and Koestler in Chapters 5 and 6 of this book.

[4] See Arthur Koestler's, *Beyond Atomism and Holism* in Chapter 6.

this physical reality is essentially mathematical in form. He thus explains the whole material world in terms of the language of mathematics, extending this principle of investigation to a universal and sweeping picture of the universe as a great machine. He treats nature as if it were the home of mathematics and the aim of science as if it were to discover the laws of the material motions that are the basis of all events. This is Monod's proclaimed Cartesianism.

*The Great Contradiction*

In Monod we see a scientist who finds in the reduction of biology and chemistry to the molecular interaction the inescapable result of scientific method. Hence the paradox of its acceptance and denial by the same man. Once again, turning to *Chance and Necessity*, let there be no mistake as to the profound character of the contradiction. Consider what he says of reason as representing an entirely new evolutionary level. He speaks of reason in man as "simulating experience subjectively so as to anticipate its result and prepare action", he describes this as the unique property of man's brain; as its remarkable "cognitive function" on which language rests; as the "creative function" of man; as entirely transcending the "calls and warnings" of animals which are not speech at all. He speaks of man's power of bringing logic to bear on experience; of "the immediate awareness of subjectivity", of "the complexity, the richness and the unfathomable depth of personal experience". He thus reaches a full recognition of what he calls, rightly, "the second evolution, that of culture", based on the unique cognitive function of the brain and the achievement of language. Following Chomsky he sees language, the innate capacity characteristic of man as a species to use a general "grammar" of language, which can translate itself into any language. It has, that is to say, an inherited neurological basis and component, but of course grammar is not chemical or physical but essentially rational and belonging to mind. In all this once again we have the full acceptance of the unique mental level so passionately denied whenever he reverts to his Cartesianism. He goes even farther and argues that "the cortical structures could not but be influenced by a capacity for language acquired very early" in man's evolution, which looks like *interactionism*; while his belief in the reality of the subjective consciousness looks like *parallelism*. Can it be that in our time these unfortunate attempts to transcend Descartes' hopeless dualism of mind and body are once more being resorted to?

So far then, from denying the second half of the Cartesian divided world, we find it once again accepted as pure mind, existing in its own right, "whose sole property it is to think", and which cannot therefore possibly exert any physical push or effect upon matter. Parallelism, which is perhaps less objectionable than interactionism, is the theory that mental processes are correlated, one to one, with processes in the brain. It isolates the psychical and the physical series of phenomena completely from each other so that neither can act on the other. They accompany each other by a blessed miracle, for, on the theory, it could not and would not make any difference to either if the other did not exist at all!

This curious theory was suited to the materialistic temper of the nineteenth century. It shelved consciousness very effectively, without exactly saying, "there is no such thing". But it is difficult to go on saying that when the ghost in the machine is breathing down your neck.

*The Cartesian Obsession*

Monod is on the horns of a dilemma, as I said at the beginning: if he considers mind as a mental entity over against the physical entity of the body, their interaction is inconceivable. In fact it would not even be possible for the mind to *perceive* the physical world let alone reason about it. But parallelism is equally an absurdity. What else? How about epiphenomenalism? Let us suppose that consciousness is an "effect", "a glow on the surface of brain matter", an exhalation itself ineffective —the steam whistle theory of consciousness. The real intention of such a theory is, of course, to exclude it from serious consideration and proceed as if there were no such thing. But if thought is only an "effect", rather unexpected consequences ensue for the validity of all thinking, including the formation and discussion of theories about brain events and books about *Chance and Necessity*. If every mental event is *basically* a physical event, a chemical process in the cortical neurones, then it is the consequence of the preceding physical state. In which case it is what it is, and cannot be judged by its fidelity to a picture of reality or by its rationality as an explanatory theory.

Thoughts, it is asserted, occur as bodily events occur, because of certain predisposing causes. These are internal to the body. A thought then, so far as causation is concerned, is on the same footing as a bodily event. Now it would be meaningless to ask whether a bodily event, the temperature of my skin for instance, was true. A statement about it must be true or false; but the temperature itself is not a statement, it simply is what it is.

Bodily events, including neural processes in the cortex, are things which occur and are real. But they are not assertions, and the question of their truth is meaningless. Now Monod's whole position is a set of ideas which purports to tell us what life and mind and the world are like. But if his theory is correct all that they tell us about is what chemical changes are taking place in his brain, and it is meaningless to say of them that they are either true or false. So Monod cannot tell us anything about the world at all. In so far as he proves his case he destroys it, for he can produce no grounds, if his theory is correct, for supposing his argument to be correct.

Are Monod and his intellectual achievements to be reduced to physics and chemistry? We are not speaking of his components which are undoubtedly none other than carbon, hydrogen, oxygen, nitrogen, sulphur, phosphorous and half a dozen other elements. But we believe his ideas are *theories*, statements *about* physical entities. Or are they to be reduced to chemical processes and nothing else? No reductionist, and no behaviourist, ever includes himself in the mechanical set up to which he reduces everyone else. G. E. Moore was amused and indignant when philosophers eloquently denying the existence of matter nevertheless knew perfectly well that they possessed solid bodies, and though questioning the reality of time were quite prepared to admit that they had had their breakfast before their lunch. Materialists are in the same position.

*The Reductive Fallacy*

It is time to attempt the solution of the problem of reconciling the inescapable fact of *difference*, with the irresistible demand for *continuity* and dependence. To resolve if we can, the paradox of scientific integrity when it requires at the same time recognition of empirical spiritual fact and of ineluctable physical law—a law system that provides none of the elements which compose the immediate experience of mankind, yet whose scheme of concepts has proved a perfect instrument for scientific research.

It comes back to Descartes, who more than any man changed the current of European thought in the seventeenth century and still holds the minds of men like Jacques Monod in thrall. He emancipated natural science from the animism with which scholastic speculation had infected it. But in treating living bodies, even the human body physically regarded, as mere machines, he set the fashion of reducing biology to physics, he created the philosophy of a universe split by its dualism into body and mind, of extramental things and intramental ideas. He claimed to have delivered philosophy from the confusions of medieval thinking by basing his whole system on indubitably clear and distinct ideas, which turned out to be so confused that ever since philosophical thought has been busy with their obscurity. No doubt that is why he has been called the father of modern philosophy.

Yet his position was justified up to a point—as a statement of the fact that physics and chemistry achieved their autonomy as sciences precisely by their emancipation from animistic and theological principles of explanation. The mechanistic theory of nature, which we call reductionism, is nothing but the triumphant declaration of this autonomy, its charter. But deepening the dualistic breach between mind and matter, it is haunted by the ghost of life and mind, afraid to admit consciousness of the uniqueness of life anywhere for fear that by conceding the principle, it may appear everywhere. By insisting on this dualism his followers have overshot anything that was necessary to check the unscientific abuse of animism as a principle of explanation. It makes its point by establishing the charter of autonomy; but it does not amount to a convincing argument for all phenomena being regarded as exclusively physico-chemical.

This all-out reductionism, especially the reduction of mental to physical phenomena, involves us in an interesting logical problem. It states that mental events are, contrary to first impressions, really only physical. If so then statements about thinking and feeling are really synonymous with statements about physical phenomena. This is more than the assertion of a correlation, which only asserts that event *A* is always accompanied by event *B*. It is an assertion to the effect that mental experiences are *nothing else* than physical events in the brain. Correlations imply distinctness and not identity, and this is not what reductionism wants.

Consider a toothache which corresponds to a decayed tooth—the physical correlative. Do we say that the only *reality* is the physical decay in the tooth? Is the pain then not real? Only real in a certain sense? Not as real as the decayed tooth? This leads us to ask what we mean by "not *really* real". Here Ayer has a useful comment.

> It is not at all clear what can be meant by saying that something is real *as an appearance*. If it is interpreted as meaning that the thing only appears to be real, then we have to conclude without qualification that it is not real. If what we mean is that the thing really appears, then we have to conclude without qualification that it is real. In neither case can we permit a half-way position.[5]

Now let us consider neural processes and thinking. If we are saying that thinking is causally dependent upon neural processes, this does not eliminate the thinking. *Ipso facto* there are two things. To say that consciousness is dependent upon brain processes is a long way from saying that it *is* brain-activity. You can know that you have a pain without knowing anything about nerve-endings. You can enjoy and understand music without knowing anything about air vibration. We may define heat as "molecules in motion" quite accurately, and this is a logical and satisfactory reduction. But that is because it is not statement about *feeling* heat. The feeling of heat cannot be reduced to molecules in motion. We cannot say it is *really* only molecules in motion. We must learn not to use the word "real" to deny the existence of anything in the world.

The question can also be considered in terms of *translation to an equivalent*, and *translation across levels*. In the first case, we translate without loss of meaning, as when we explain boiling as the change of water from its liquid state to water vapour at a higher temperature. Translation *with* loss of meaning is when we explain toothache entirely in terms of physical decay, which loses the meaning associated with excruciating pain. Translation across levels requires the *separate identifiability* of the terms, e.g., the stimulation of taste buds on the tongue on the one hand and the taste of sweetness on the other. Similarly we cannot say that *red* is merely vibration of a certain wavelength; that is not the equivalent even if it is a translation, because it crosses from one level to an entirely different one. Neither can we translate life in all its richness, and mind in its infinite variety, to a level which is essentially molecular.

Monod fails to understand this argument, insisting that translation means equivalence, and therefore, since thought has its neurological correlate, it must be translated into neural events and nothing

[5] A. J. Ayer, *Metaphysics and Common Sense*.

else. Any suggestion that new functions with their own reality and their own principles arise on the level of life and mind, he rejects as animism or vitalism.

But at the same time he accepts the unique qualities of both life and mind on the basis of "its unique and irrefutable witness to itself".

> What doubt can there be of the presence of the spirit within us? To give up the illusion that sees in it an immaterial substance is not to deny the existence of the soul, but on the contrary to begin to recognize its complexity.[6]

This is a complete return to Descartes's fundamental dualism, the recognition of the existence of spiritual being on the ground of the *cogito*—"I think, therefore I am". Monod never attempts to justify his belief in the spiritual world on rational grounds. He appeals only to existential choice as its basis, and to arbitrary ethical postulates as the basis of morals and social life. This is hardly different from Descartes's "clear and distinct ideas," which turned out to have far less certainty than Descartes imagined. Their basis is only what this man or that man *feels* to be indubitable. It is to fall back on the pure subjectivity which, in the words of Jacques Maritain, has been:

> The source of the torrent of illusions and fables which have poured upon us for 250 years, making the mind itself the measure of what *is*.[7]

Monod makes no attempt to justify his intuition or existential choice, and by failing to do so identifies himself with those who believe in inspiration; dictators, prophets, medicine men, fortune tellers and astrologers, gypsies, and the Word of God. Subjectivism is complete. Relativist existentialism is the order of the day. Make a free decision, commit yourself to the oracle you like, or obey the oracle that has chosen you. In Monod's own words this "is not a judgment reached from knowledge". It does not impose itself on man as the recognition of any objective reality, "on the contrary, it is he who imposes it on himself".

Where now is Monod's faith in the sole authority of objective knowledge? It has been abandoned for total subjectivity.

[6] J. Monad, *Chance and Necessity*.
[7] Jacques Maritain, *Trois reformateurs*, Paris, 1925.

## *Part II: The Fallacy of Misplaced Concreteness*

Where then are we to find the objective ground for the spiritual life of man which Monod, likes the rest of us, feels compelled to recognise? Can it not be shown that since mind is not a stuff, a substance of the same category as matter, its reality consists in its being a function of a certain kind of matter, namely the brains of men, and indeed of the human organism as a whole, the undeniable thinking, feeling and valuing man. But to grasp this we have to see that science by its own method, and to achieve its own important object, must limit its form of knowledge to a good deal less than the whole of reality.

The physicist *for his purposes* may define red in terms of wave-length, but this cannot diminish or subtract from what exists. He may legitimately ignore the sensation because it is his business to study the physical conditions and not the sensations. But we do not *see* the wave-length, we see red. The physicist is giving us some useful information when he states the conditions which make it possible to see red, but he is not reducing the sensation to these conditions.

But it is easier for the layman to find no difficulty in believing that life is only complicated chemistry than for him to believe that because the grooves on his gramophone record (which are physical and measurable) are necessary for him to hear the sonata, the music actually *is* the physical series of grooves and nothing more; that the cathedral is *only* a pile of stones, that the "man only an enormous number of interacting molecules". But he is wrong; just as in the case of the cathedral the structure, the design, the significance, the artistic quality are as real as the stones, but more significant. Man is more than the sum of his parts, more than an aggregate of cells, and is all that the history of the world has shown him capable of, both in greatness and in littleness, in goodness and in wickedness, in ingenuity, rational thought and artistic achievement. All these characteristics are as real as his constituent molecules.

Perhaps biologists who are reductionist in their views protect themselves from a clear realisation of this by keeping their work mainly to the non-human field and dealing in physical principles equally applicable to the non-human and the human, the inanimate and the animate. But what the reductionist has really been doing is to select, to abstract, for his purposes that aspect of a complex reality which it is his special business to examine, in exactly the same way as when I step on a weighing machine and the dial reads 11 st. 4 lbs., I am selecting my weight from all my other properties and characteristics. That is a measureable aspect of the person, and may be for medical reasons an important one, but it is not a description of the concrete whole. To regard the abstraction of physico-chemical aspects as the reality at last, is to commit the fallacy of misplaced concreteness. The abstraction is at farthest remove from concrete reality.

*The Abstract and the Concrete*

An immense range of sheer fact can be by-passed legitimately if the intention is to deal with one particular aspect. The physicist's world is not the entire world of nature, and his findings do not in any way restrict that world to the limits of what he has chosen to deal with. It is the physicist's world that is so restricted, not *the* world, and clearly his methods are not adequate to the description of all that can be found in it. Physics necessarily becomes abstract because by its own decision it makes use exclusively of mathematical concepts and the limitations this imposes on its knowledge. The danger is to take notions and concepts which are valid for this perspective and apply them uncritically to another.

It is here that philosophy should come in to make clear the interrelation of different modes of understanding existence. Philosophy surveys all such abstractive systems with the special function of their harmony and their completion; above all it confronts the sciences with concrete fact.

In the process of selection the further you go in seeking what is common to everything, the more you leave out of account; and of course the more *general* is your outlook. It appears luminously clear to many people, especially those who like broad general principles explaining a multitude of facts, that the general truths which cover the most ground, must be the most complete, the most comprehensive and exhaustive. What is the one basic explanation of *all* wars? Of crime? Of mental disorders? Of economic instability? The final explanation, the one general principle is eagerly sought: "aggression" of course "the hereditary factor" for criminality, Freud's subconscious"— "capitalism". There we go! And now, what is the ultimate ground of the universe? Why, atoms in motion of course; or, if you are a mentalist, just Mind and its manifestation; both completely wrong—both forms of the higher lunacy!

For the wider the generalisation, the more differing particulars it covers (and ignores), the greater the diversity which is reduced to a unity by abstracting what is common to them all. And in science, which we all know is the only objective, rational and experimental truth, order, unity, must consist in principles of *one* kind, and the only universal scientific systematisation of one kind is the physico-chemical.

But does maximising the general really give us unified knowledge? It can only lead to abstraction, to levelling, or assimilating, differences which ought to be recognised in their characteristic uniqueness and retained in an order of superimposed levels. The physico-chemical analysis of living things *includes* the living in the wider general class by ignoring precisely what is characteristically living about them. The differences are swallowed up in "another case of the same sort".

It is refreshing when the monist who wants everything comprised in one basic principle is confronted with a pluralist like Bertrand Russell:

> The most fundamental of my intellectual beliefs is that the idea that the world is a unity is rubbish. I think the universe is all spots and jumps, without unity and without continuity, without coherence or orderliness, or any of the other properties that governesses love.[8]

"It takes all sorts to make a world." There are other universals than *the widest* type of generality. These are the genuine entities we call wholes, systems, especially living organisms, into which the ultimate elements, beloved by the monist with his one universal stuff, enter as constituents, and make real, complex unities with new properties. Complete analysis is not enough. New levels of phenomena have to be recognised and dealt with on their own terms.

The completely general, the molecular, is only reached by the ignoring, or levelling of differences, while emphasis on "wholes" is characteristic of concrete philosophy. True thinking will go the way not of abstraction but synthesis. Analysis hypostatises the abstractions, making the non-self-sufficient into the self-sufficient. Instead of finding

[8] *The Philosophy of Bertrand Russell*, (ed.) Paul A. Schilpp. Bertrand Russell is not a maverick philosopher by any means, and his pluralism is shared by many others notably G. E. Moore, William James, F. C. S. Schiller, R. B. Perry, and Jean Wahl.

the concrete where it really is, in the fullness of experience, analysis mistakenly believes that it has found it in a partial aspect of reality. It is here that philosophy corrects the one-sidedness of scientific thinking, especially mathematically orientated science.

The sciences use their own set of concepts, select their own aspects, what is to be real for them. Every method becomes a net to catch only fish of a certain size, the rest are allowed to get through. But press Monod's reductionist principle far enough and ultimately the world will be found to be not molecular but a complex of metrical symbols. Eddington some years ago wrote a popular but alarming book[9] which translated molecules into electrons and then assured us that the firm plank we proposed to step on was *really* more unsubstantial than a swarm of gnats. It had no solidity and it would be a perilous venture on it. Matter was becoming more and more tenuous; until, in the form which we have always taken for granted, it disappeared altogether. It was a philosopher who pointed out that the world of solid planks still stood and retained its full reality.[10] The electronic world was not *the* world but the abstract world of modern physics; and it could cease to be even electronic tomorrow and dissolve into something beyond all imaginable models, into mathematical symbols perhaps. But even if it did, it would leave the concrete world exactly where it was; all that the physicist has done as far as the familiar world is concerned is to cut nature down to fit into the framework of laws of his own choosing.[11]

Perhaps the reason why the reductionist cannot imagine life except as an intrusion from without is because he is at heart a Cartesian dualist, believing in two distinct realities physical substance and mental substance. If he did not himself conceive of life as an entity and mind as necessarily a spiritual substance he would not insist that every claim that *this* is living, or *that* is thinking, is a claim that the non-natural, some non-physical entity, has intruded into the closed physical world. It is because life *must* be a thing in itself, that everyone who insists that an organism is living *must* be an animist, and that living processes *must* be dissociated from other natural processes. He would not raise the question of vitalist heresy, nor would he eliminate life, if he did not believe in the first plea, unconsciously, that it is a mysterious thing

[9] Eddington, *The Nature of the Physical World.*
[10] Stebbing, *Philosophy and the Physicists.*
[11] No one is denying the legitimacy and importance of doing so, provided the scientist does not extrapolate physics to a metaphysical absolute—which is not being scientific.

which intervenes in the processes of physical existence, and that it is this mystery that every one who is not a reductionist must be trying to put over. Hence the desperate anxiety to treat every alternative to complete reductionism as a nefarious attempt to betray the cause of objectivity.

Monod describes these theories as holding that physics and chemistry "do not fully account for the properties of living things". Hence it must be accepted that certain principles, which become *added* to those of physics, are operative in living matter. He refers to the views of Polanyi and Elsassar and argues that "the reductionist attitude is doomed to fail in its attempt to reduce the properties of a very complex organization to the 'sum' of the properties of its parts". He finds the evidence for this in the theories of L. Bertalanffy, Paul Weiss, Arthur Koestler, C. H. Waddington, Jean Piaget, J. R. Smythies W. H. Thorpe and other contributors to the symposium *Beyond Reductionism*. But, of course, none of these could reasonably be regarded as accepting any form of vitalism or animism. By saddling all his opponents with such indefensible theories he has no difficulty, of course, in refuting them; but in this way he also systematically avoids ever having to confront their criticism of his position. John Stuart Mill once said:

> It is the most reasonable rather than the absurdest form of one's opponent's opinion with which one ought to grapple. We stand little chance of discovering what truth such opinions may contain if we merely attack their weaker aspects.[12]

Perhaps a disciple of Descartes and an apostle of objectivity will not be unwilling to learn from an English rationalist a better method of scientific debate.

Because he fails to do so it is hardly surprising to find Monod choosing the "vulgar Marxism" which sees society as carried irresistibly forward on an immanent dialectical wave of progress to criticise as animistic rather than the Marxism of Marx who explicitly repudiated any such theory.[13]

Of course, Monod knows perfectly well that he is not criticising Marx at all but some distortion or perversion of it now current. As

[12] B. Willey, *Nineteenth-Century Studies*.

[13] "It is never possible to arrive at understanding by using the *passe-partout* of some historical-philosophical theory whose great virtue is to stand above history." *Marx and Engels Works*, Vol. XV, 378.

he himself says "one may well say that this version does not reflect Marx's own idea and is a relatively late addition to the socio-economic edifice which Marx had already raised". If so why call it Marxism?

It would have been interesting to learn what Monod would have made of the views of contemporary Marxist scholars whose works are widely read and discussed in Paris today. One might mention Merleau-Ponty, Lukacs, Korsch, Lefebvre, Schmidt and Lichtheim; but he appears not to be disposed to discuss the theories of the real Marx but only those of his less responsible and less scholarly epigones.

## *Part III: The Category Mistake*

The reductionist finds it impossible to see this because he is convinced that this way of putting the situation implies that the "function" and "principles" ascribed to living things must mean that they represent the properties of a non-physical substance or force. To consider life as real is to put the phenomenon into the *category* of physical existents. To say that thought is real is to consider it to be a *thing*, an object, like the brain itself, an entity of the same type. Existence, he assumes, has to be *like* that of bodily material objects. *It belongs to that category*, and that is why he rejects it if applied to life or mind. And if it were so he would be right to do so. But it is not. It claims to be *real* in a different category, as a *mode* of being, in Aristotelian terms: "As sight is to the eye, thought is to the brain"—and it is *real*. Sight is real although it is not in the same category as *eye*. It is not real as a physical object, and does not have to be a physical object in order to claim reality. Nor does it cease to be real when it is discovered not to be in that category. Nor is someone who does claim that it is real, saying that it has that kind of reality. If he did, he would be animistic.

In exactly the same way there can be explanations which are not in the same category as physical explanation, and both can operate at once, just as gravity and magnetic attraction can operate together and prevent a piece of metal from falling. We may consider a chess move as a purely physical movement, abstracting it from everything else in the situation; but it can also be a move according to the rules of chess. One and the same process can be compatible with two principles of completely different types, and such that neither is reducible to the other, though one of them presupposes and depends on the other. Billiard balls go where mechanical forces make them go; but they also go at the same time, where the player wants them to go. But knowledge and skill of the player does not contradict and is not inconsistent with physical laws. This asks for no suspension of mechanical laws, no exception, no *impact* of mind on muscle or ball. The reductionist view assumes that an action of this sort could not be judged mentally unless it were an exception to scientific understanding. But the billiard player does not ask for the suspension of the laws of nature in order to exercise his skill.[14]

There is no need for a desperate salvage operation to withdraw actions governed by purpose from the physical world and place them in another where mind rules. No occult intervention is required for actions to be mind controlled, or morally motivated.

Neither life nor mind is being explained by the opponents of reductionism as a ghost harnessed to a machine. That is not what they mean—and it is beside the point for Monod to insist that it is. It *is*, of course, for a Cartesian. But they are not Cartesians.

Ryle gives an excellent illustration of the laws of two separate categories operating simultaneously when he considers the writing of a work of history like Gibbon's *Decline and Fall:*

> "It may well be that throughout the whole length of *The Decline and Fall of the Roman Empire* Gibbon never once infringes the rules of English grammar. They governed his entire writing, yet they did not ordain what he should write, or even the style in which he should write, they merely forbade certain ways of conjoining words . . . An argumentative passage from the *Decline and Fall* might be examined for the grammatical rules which it observes. There is no conflict or competition between these different types of principles; all alike are applied in the same material. . . .
>
> (Similarly) the discoveries of the physical sciences no more rule out life, sentience, purpose or intelligence from presence in the world than do the rules of grammar extrude style or logic from prose. Certainly the physical sciences say nothing of life, but nor do the rules of grammar say anything about history.

[14] Gilbert Ryle, *The Concept of Mind.*

> For the laws of physics apply to what is animate as well as to what is inanimate, just as the rules of grammar apply to *Whitaker's Almanac* as well as to *The Decline and Fall*, to Mrs. Eddy's as well as to Hume's reasonings."[15]

This is the crux of the argument between reductionists and objective thinkers. It applies just as much to the levels in biology, to the autonomy and distinctiveness and *validity* of biochemical laws, Mendelian laws, the laws of populations in evolution, the laws of thought, and the laws of harmony in music, in relation to the molecular substratum to which they cannot be reduced without remainder.

The laws of a higher stage cannot be reduced to, or predicted from, or treated as particular cases of, the more general laws of a lower stage. Scientists themselves if they work in the field of biology or even chemistry do not have to work with theories of pure mechanism. In all cases the physical laws define the limits within which all possible motions fall, but they do not determine *that* any particular motion happens, or *when*, or in detail the *way in which* one motion will be different from other motions, one motion will be concerned with sound and another with heat and another with the chemistry of a cortical neurone.

*The Autonomy of the Biological Sciences*

Let us take as an example the current explanation of the breakdown of carbohydrates to release energy for vital processes in the organism. In view of Monod's helpful use of diagrams to make clear his molecular theories, perhaps I may be allowed to use the same method to demonstrate the autonomy of biochemistry in oxidation, showing a long chain of processes, involving a regular build-back of the substances concerned at many points in the cycle.

*The Krebs' Cycle*

This shows the breakdown of pyruvic acid to carbon dioxide and water during which process its energy reserves are transferred to the ATP batteries. The pyruvic and similar acids all enter into the complex sequence of events which constitute the Krebs' cycle, which begins and ends with oxaloacetic acid. The pyruvic acid is "carried" round this cycle by the oxaloacetic acid and finally converted into carbon

[15] Gilbert Ryle, *The Concept of Mind* (slightly abridged).

dioxide and water. Some of the steps are oxidations during which energy is transferred to ADP. The last oxidation results in the formation of oxaloacetic acid, ready once again to carry pyruvic acid round the cycle.

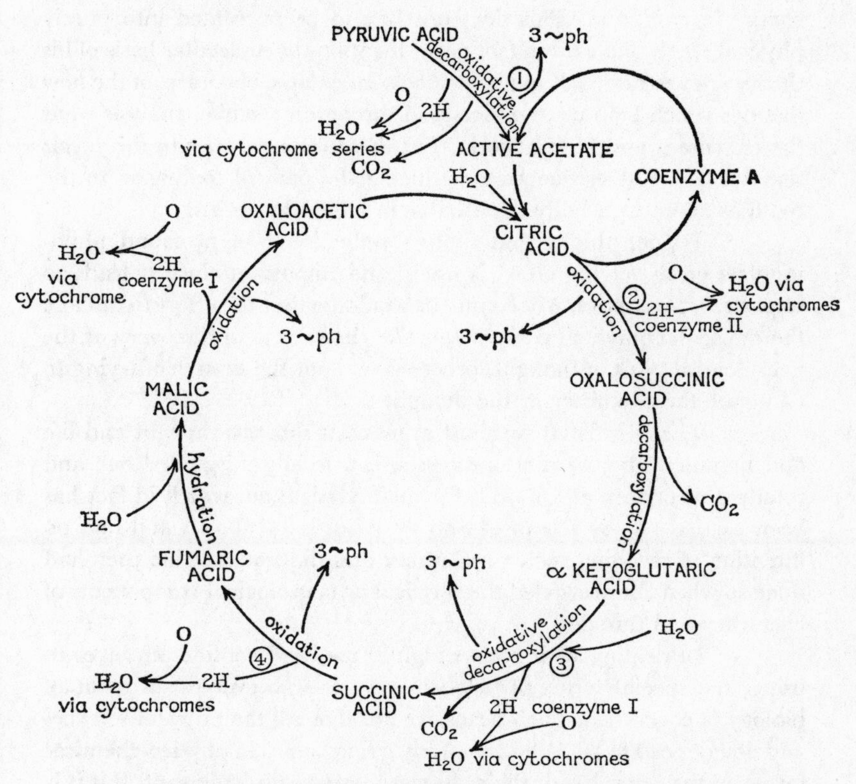


Krebs cycle. Each ~ ph formed converts one molecule of ADP to ATP.

When oxidations occur, they are brought about by the removal of hydrogen. The essential requirements for each successive oxidative stage are therefore the presence of the appropriate enzyme and of a hydrogen acceptor to receive the hydrogen.

All this can be and is always described and explained *in chemical terms* and this is sufficient for all biochemical and biological purposes. It is not unreal, or illusory, or in need of reduction to the molecular level to be perfectly correct.[16]

The biochemist takes his concepts and laws and processes as completely valid in their own right. He can explain precisely the complex chemical processes involved in photosynthesis or the liberation of energy in oxidation. This does not *have* to be translated into purely physical terms. He may in fact never mention the molecular basis of his theory or even discuss it in his textbook. He knows, of course, of the new theories which help us to understand through molecular analysis what the enzyme is and how it works. But there is no *reduction* to this level; that would be as erroneous as reducing the pain of toothache to the tooth as an entity wholly describable in molecular terms.

Popper thinks that though reduction is a profound philosophical error yet the effort is useful and important since it leads to important discoveries. My comment would be that the effort to disclose the molecular physical component, like the successful discovery of the neurological basis of thought, proceeds without the motive of trying to eliminate the chemistry or the thought.

The belief that we must at all costs *eliminate* thought and life and its unique biochemical processes, is a totally misguided one and totally unnecessary as a motive for the investigation, which in fact has been carried out by scientists who were not reductionists and had no intention of reaching such conclusions, and did not imagine they had done so when they revealed the physical or neurological components of chemistry and thinking.

In dealing with life we rightly use, and confine ourselves to using, the special terms of biochemistry, or whatever department of biology is concerned. Such terms are not those of the physical sciences and do not need to be. When we study living beings in physico-chemical terms on the other hand, their character as *living* is irrelevant. But it is neither explained nor rejected, it is simply in this context ignored. It is no part of the physicist's universe of discourse. The concept of life, then, is a distinct concept, of a different order from physical or chemical concepts, and not reducible to them.

To consider the uniqueness as "super-natural" or "animistic" whether this is the view of a vitalist *or a reductionist*, is simply a category mistake. "Living" is not a category within which we group physical

[16] The fact that it can be is, of course, not unimportant and is perfectly legitimate, but does not eliminate the chemistry.

motion and chemical motion, as processes of a kind. When it appears it is as a process and a function, prepared for (as Monod so ably shows) by a series of stages leading up to the leap to novelty which brings it into existence in the world of evolution. It is not an *addition* to the purely physical stage which preceded it, and *in the same category*. It is a new function of matter at a higher level of organisation.

*The Reassertion of Mind*

One thing further needs to be said. Monod believes that he is able to reduce life to mechanism: but he fails and he knows he fails to do this with mind. Hence when he reaches man, since he cannot without losing his reason insist that all the thoughts and hopes and achievements of man are only molecules in motion, what *does* he *do*? He becomes a 100 per cent animist, a dualist, he postulates mind as existing in its own right and making existential choices to establish all sorts of metaphysical principles, including a series of ethical postulates on which he hopes to base socialism and construct a moral order.

On the basis of the hierarchy of functions we are arguing for it is, of course, possible without recourse to blind commitment to take care of all the categories of social and ethical life, and discuss the formation of criteria and the processes of *rational* criticism on which their validity depends. To this and to the further discussion of the *limits* of physico-chemical explanation we shall return in subsequent chapters.

But first we have to see just how, while remaining wholly within the limits of the natural sciences, we may yet take account of the processes, distinguishing qualities, and regularities entirely beyond the limits of mechanism. This has been persuasively argued by the organistic biologists who will put their case in the next two chapters.

Monod is aware of their position but dismisses it as a return to animism. He seems unaware that in their view the molecular basis for the higher levels is not questioned, nor is exhaustive analysis to penetrate this basis rejected—though he, and others who share his attitude, always say so. Monod imagines, without any grounds for doing so, that organicists like Polanyi, Needham, Koestler and Bertalanffy refuse to recognise the unique though still purely mechanical basis of the higher levels and do not wish these interactions to be investigated. This is nonsense. What they do argue is that although the mechanical and chemical levels continue into the higher levels, which are dependent on them, the structures and processes of these levels are unique and are biological, and at a higher level mental.

It must be because Monod always thinks, with the unstated presupposition that the natural world can only contain physical events, that when it is claimed that there are living phenomena and mental phenomena, that must be an assertion of the intrusion of a mental or animistic *substance*. But that assumption is simply the consequence of his Cartesian dualism. For the organicist there is only one world and it contains objective realities of a mechanical, chemical, biological and psychological kind, and also all the undeniable realities of human culture and values. They are not idealists; for them the world is not in the mind but the mind is in the world.

Polanyi has convincingly shown by his principles of boundary control that the physical laws cease explaining the phenomena beyond their own limits. The physical description can be exhaustive and yet never reach the entities and laws of the higher level, as in the case of the grooves on a record and the actual music, which is neither illusory nor can it be described in physical terms. This does not mean that the physical laws cease to operate here or that their operation on this level is beyond analysis, but however far you analyse it you never reach the psychological and aesthetic. A painting can be analysed exclusively in terms of the chemical constituents of the colours; cobalt, chrome, iron and so forth; but however far you push your analysis you will never reach on this level either the unique experience of colour, or the aesthetic qualities of the picture. Does Monod really deny the objectivity of the colour red? If pressed he might say that it existed only in consciousness —a clear collapse into the dualism that accepts consciousness as a Cartesian substance having no existence in space and whose sole property it is *to think*. This is not the position of the organicist, for whom consciousness is as much a real property of persons as their physical and chemical existence. There is no mysticism or animism in including within our *one* world both its indispensable and universal basis of physical and chemical entities and interactions *and* all the richness and complexity of the higher levels of human experience, all of them beyond the limits of physical description.

To this problem Joseph Needham and Arthur Koestler will address themselves immediately.

CHAPTER FIVE

# *Integrative Levels and the Idea of Progress*

JOSEPH NEEDHAM

The theme of integrative levels is not one which we can approach without considerable hesitation, since the field which it covers is so wide and deep, no less than the whole nature of the world we know, and the way in which it has come into being. No one thinker can hope to do justice to this theme, and the only apology which may be offered for treating of it is that interest must always attach to what a specialist in any field of research may say when he abandons for a moment his speciality and looks boldly out to consider the world. Moreover, in taking the whole world for one's province, one may the more easily, though a scientist, escape the condemnation of philosophers, who, ever since Plato, have been rather interested in the world as a whole. The subject, then, to which our attention is to be given is the existence of levels of organisation in the universe, successive forms of order in a scale of complexity and organisation. The cosmological changes which eventually produced a number of worlds, probably rather small among the galaxies, suitable for the existence of massed and complicated carbon compounds in the colloidal state, have become a commonplace background of our thought. So also the conception of biological evolution, in the course of which the many-celled animals and the plants arose from single-celled organisms probably somewhat resembling the autotrophic bacteria of today. A sharp change in organisational level often means that what were wholes on the lower level become parts on the new, e.g., protein crystals in cells, cells in metazoan organisms, and metazoan organisms in social units. Lastly, the anthropologists and ethnologists have familiarised all of us with the idea of evolutionary development in sociology, where we see the gradual development of human communities from the earliest beginnings of social relationships to the conception of the co-operative commonwealth now dawning upon the world.

But this great sweep of vision needs further elucidation. First, if we look carefully at the steps between the successive levels of organisation we find that the sharp lines of distinction are only made all the more sharp by the "mesoforms" which occur between them. Thus between living and non-living matter the realm of the crystalline represents the highest degree of organisation of which non-living matter is capable. It approaches, moreover, quite closely to the realm of the living in the phenomena presented by the so-called "liquid crystals", states of matter intermediate between the random orientation of a liquid and the almost absolute rigidity of the true crystal. These "paracrystals", with their internal structure and their directional properties, are closely related to living systems. Living systems, indeed, almost certainly contain many components of a paracrystalline nature. The viruses again, minute ultramicroscopic particles, probably represent some kind of intermediate form between living and lifeless. But these forms of existence, the more clearly we understand them, will all the more clearly serve to bring out the essentially new elements of higher order which characterise the form of organisation we call life.

Secondly, there follows from the developmental nature of social organisation a conclusion which some thinkers, though otherwise clear minded, have not been so ready to see, namely, that we have no reason to suppose that our present condition of civilisation is the last masterpiece of universal organisation, the highest form of order of which nature is capable. On the contrary, there are many grounds for seeing in collectivism a form of organization as much above the *manière d'être* of middle-class nations as their form of order was superior to that of primitive tribes. It would hardly be going too far to say that the transition from economic individualism to the common ownership of the world's productive resources by humanity is a step similar in nature with the transition from lifeless proteins to the living cell, or from primitive savagery to the first community, so clear is the continuity between inorganic, biological and social order. Thus, on such a view, the future state of social justice is seen to be no fantastic Utopia, no desperate hope, but a form of organisation having the whole force of evolution behind it. But the acceptance of this implies a certain revaluation of the idea of progress. The idea of progress as applied to biological and social evolution fell into great discredit as the result of Victorian optimism. It was pointed out that evolution has often been regressive, that parasitism has been a widespread phenomenon in biology, and that before speaking of progress in evolution we should consider "the hookworm's point of view". Nevertheless, apart from the fact that the hookworm's nervous system does not entitle it to have a point of view, we cannot seriously bring ourselves to refuse to apply the concepts of higher and lower organisation to the animal world. Vertebrates *are*, in general, of higher organisation than invertebrates, mammals than other vertebrates, and human beings than other mammals. Again, in social affairs the vast miseries caused by industrialisation and modern warfare were set against the doubtfully happier conditions of ancient times, and pessimistic conclusions adverse to the conception of progress were easily reached. But the time-scale was here insufficient; the exceedingly short space of time during which human civilisation has existed as compared with the time taken in biological evolution was forgotten. Post-Victorian pessimism mistook the development of a certain phase for the whole of progress itself. Of a famous Edwardian statesman it was said that he approached politics with the air of one who remembered that there had once been an ice age and that it was very likely there would be another. He was unnecessarily chilly. In the light of biology and sociology those who remember that there were once autotrophic bacteria and that there will some day be a co-operative commonwealth of the human totality are better politicians.

## TIME AND THE BIOLOGISTS

Since biochemistry is the most borderline of sciences, it is only natural that a biochemist should devote a good deal of attention to its philosophical position. That chemistry should indeed be able to cover the realms both of the inanimate and the animate was a fact quite sufficiently a riddle in itself. The whole history of biochemistry, indeed, has been the scene of a persistent debate between those who have taken the hopeful view that the phenomena of life would one day be fully explicable in physico-chemical terms, and those who have thought themselves able to see in these phenomena evidences of some guiding influence—*spiritus rector, archaeus, vis formativa*, entelechy, or what you will—formally impossible to bring into relation with chemistry. Often enough these "vitalists", as they have been called, not content with prognostications of failure, have purported to give proofs, of a more or less convincing nature, that the phenomena of life must ever resist scientific explanation.[1] During the first three decades of the present century the majority of working biologists and biochemists were not "vitalists" but "mechanists". About 1928 their position could fairly justly be summed up as follows:

> "Mechanists do not say that nothing is true or intelligible unless expressed in physico-chemical terms, they do not say that nothing takes place differently in living matter from what takes place in dead, they do not say that our present physics and chemistry are fully competent to explain the behaviour of living systems. What they do say is that the processes of living matter are subject to the same laws which govern the processes of dead matter, but that the laws operate in a more complicated medium; thus living things differ from dead things in degree and not in kind, and are, as it were, *extrapolations* from the inorganic."[2]

But the nature of the extrapolation was still obscure. The question entered a new phase, however, with the publication of J. H. Woodger's remarkable book *Biological Principles*.[3] There it was laid down that the term "vitalism" should thenceforward be restricted to all propositions of the type "the living being consists of an X *in addition to* carbon, hydrogen, oxygen, nitrogen, etc., *plus organizing relations*". Recognition of the objectivity and importance of organising relations had always been an empirical necessity, forced upon biologists by the very subject-matter of their science, but the issue was always confused by their inability to distinguish between the *organisation* of the living system and its supposed *anima*. With the abolition of souls and vital forces the genuine organising relations in the organism could become the object of scientific study. Before the contribution of Woodger, "organicism", as it had been called, had necessarily been of an obscurantist character, since it was supposed, as, for example, by J. S. Haldane, that the organising relations were themselves the *anima*, and as such inscrutable to scientific analysis. Today we are perfectly clear (though a few

[1] Such as Hans Driesch in his *Science and Philosophy of the Organism*, London, 1908.
[2] J. Needham, *The Sceptical Biologist*, London, 1929, p. 247.
[3] London, 1929.

biologists may still fail to appreciate this point) that the organisation of living systems is the problem, not the axiomatic starting-point, of biological research. Organising relations exist, but they are not immune from scientific grasp and understanding. On the other hand, their laws are not likely to be reducible to the laws governing the behaviour of molecules at lower levels of complexity. It would be correct to say that the living differs from the dead in degree and not in kind because it is on a higher plane of complexity of organisation, but it would also be correct to say that it differs in kind, since the laws of this higher organisation only operate there. On closer examination good instances of the Hegelian conception of the passing of quantity into quality could probably be found in this region.

It may be of use to follow a little further the difference between the older dogmatic organicism and the new point of view. Organisation is inscrutable, it was urged, since any organic part instantly loses its relational properties on removal from the whole, and no means are available for rendering the wholes transparent so that we can observe them while intact. But fortunately these statements are not true. Woodger[4] has distinguished three main possibilities in the relation of organic part to organic whole: (*a*) independence; (*b*) functional dependence; (*c*) existential dependence. A part of the first sort would pursue its normal activities independently of whether it was in connection with its normal whole or not. A part of the second sort would be disorganised, if so isolated, and a part of the third sort would cease even to be recognisable. Dogmatic organicists, ignoring these distinctions, assumed that all parts are parts of the third sort. Yet this is certainly not the case. Liver cells synthesise glycogen and iris cells melanin in tissue culture as well as in the body. Isolated enzyme systems carry out their multifarious reactions in extracts as well as in the intact cells. Even existential dependence is a difficulty which can be overcome if means exist for making wholes "transparent", as by X-ray analysis of membranes or fibres, examination of living cells in polarising microscopes or ultraviolet spectrometers, or by "marking" in-going molecules by substituting isotope elements in them, such as heavy hydrogen or phosphorus.

It was a striking fact that in other countries other biologists had been coming to similar conclusions. In Russia, under the guidance of an elaborate philosophy at that time almost unknown here, a new

[4] *Proc. Aristot. Soc.*, 1932, xxxii, 117.

organicism had been growing up, but so little were English men of science prepared for it that the very sensible and elaborate communications of the Russian delegation to the International Congress for the History of Science at the Science Museum at South Kensington, London, in 1931, were received with bewilderment.

> "The true task of scientific research," said Zawadowsky, "is not the violent identification of the biological and the physical, but the discovery of the qualitatively specific controlling principles which characterize the main features of every phenomenon, and the finding of methods of research appropriate to the phenomena studied. . . . It is necessary to renounce both the simplified reduction of some sciences to others, and also the sharp demarcations between the physical, biological, and socio-historical sciences."

Again, in a passage which indicates a point of view closely similar to that already outlined, he writes:

> "Biological phenomena, historically connected with physical phenomena in inorganic nature, are none the less not only not reducible to physico-chemical or mechanical laws, but within their own limits as biological processes display different and qualitatively distinct laws. But biological laws do not in the least lose thereby their material quality and cognizability, requiring only in each case methods of research appropriate to the phenomena studied."

Or, in other words, biological order is both comprehensible and different from inorganic order. In France similar views have been put forward, as, for instance, by Marcel Prenant, also in accordance with the indications of materialist dialectics. This philosophy has been called the profoundest theory of natural evolution, the theory of the nature of transformations, and the origin of the qualitatively new, indeed, the natural methodology of science itself. It was striking to find that its conclusions upon a point of the most fundamental interest to the biochemist, the meaning of the transition from the dead to the living, should coincide with those which he had worked out independently by sincerely following the dictates of scientific commonsense.

The question had always been particularly serious for those

biochemists who interested themselves in the problems of morphology. The enzymes involved in metabolism may be isolated and studied in relatively simple systems, analyses may be made of the substances entering and leaving the living body, even the blood and tissue fluids may be examined in relation to every conceivable bodily activity, change, or disease—but all this avoids the main problem of biology, the origin, nature and maintenance of specific organic structure. The building of a bridge between biochemical and morphological concepts is perhaps the most important task before biologists at the present time, and it may well be long before it is satisfactorily accomplished. But in the course of the present century several branches of study of great value in this connection have sprung up, particularly in embryology, where the changing organic form is the most obvious variable during development. Experimental and chemical embryology together have made much progress towards the unification of chemical and morphological concepts. But this impressive change of morphological form takes place along the time-axis. In the development of the individual organism, as in that of organisms in general, progression takes place from low to high complexity, from inferior to superior organisation. There had been a time when a certain level of organisation had not existed, there would come a time when higher levels would appear. Time is again the inevitable datum.

Let us now take another look at the giant vista which has all along been the background of our thoughts. The stage once prepared by cosmic evolution for the appearance of life, what follows shows an ever-rising level of organisation. The number of parts in the wholes increases, as also the complexity of their structure and their interrelations, the centralisation and efficiency of the means of control (whether humoral or neural), and the flexibility and versatility of their actions on the external environment. The wholes become, indeed, ever more independent of the external environment; by regulation of exchanges in energy and materials an interior equilibrium is doggedly maintained, and though death destroys it in the individual it continues in the species. If we run through any biological textbook we find abundant illustrations of this. Although some of the paracrystals already mentioned show a degree of complexity which seems to approach that of the simplest living organisms, it is the autotrophic bacteria which first exhibit the basic phenomena of the new level, reproduction and metabolism. They were (and are today) able to synthesise all the carbon compounds needed for their architecture from the carbon dioxide of the atmosphere by the aid of energy obtained from oxidations of inorganic substances (iron, sulphur, etc.). The many kinds of parasitic bacteria with which most of us are more familiar are to be supposed a regression from these primitive forms. But all was not regression, for by another big step cells grew enormously larger and the protozoa came into being. Some of these developed the photosynthetic mechanism, others did not. The former, when united together in colonies, became the first plants, the latter, similarly co-operating, became the first animals. Then began that long procession of morphological forms and physiological achievements which the biologists have charted, with all its turning-points, the first coelomic organisation, the first endocrine mechanism, the first osmo-regulatory success, the first vertebral column, the first appearance of consciousness, the first making of a tool. At the point at which social life begins, factors set in so new as to constitute a recognisably higher level. Rational control of the environment now for the first time becomes a possibility. About the first beginnings of social organisation we know rather less than about some of the earlier, biological stages. It is doubtful how far our consideration of humanity's problems can be assisted by a knowledge of the phenomena of social life in ants and bees (the social hymenoptera), for the anatomical nature of these animals, with its exoskeleton and rather inferior nervous system, is so far removed from our own. The behaviour of the sub-human Primates has much more to tell us, but even that, as Zuckerman points out, does not tell us much. Man's precursors probably lived a social life similar to that of all old-world monkeys and apes and were probably frugivorous. Probably at the beginning of the Pliocene, some 20,000,000 years ago, when forests were reduced and the earth became more arid, a group of Primates with more plastic food-habits than the rest managed to survive by becoming carnivorous. This transfer from a grazing to a hunting life must have had important social and sexual consequences, for with the change of diet there had to go a sexual division of labour in food collection. Hence there had to be a repression of the dominant impulses which lead to polygyny in sub-human Primates.

> "The price of our emergence as Man," writes Zuckerman, "would seem to have been the overt renunciation of a dominant Primate impulse in the field of sex. The price of our continued

> existence may well be further repressions of dominant impulses, and *further developments* of the co-operative behaviour whose beginnings can be vaguely seen in our transition from a simian to a human level of existence."

Every transition from the unconscious to the conscious implies a step from bondage to freedom, from lower to higher level of organisation. All early agriculture and storage of food-products necessitated more conscious control than before. Increases in the efficiency of mechanisms of transport from the horse to the aeroplane widened men's conscious horizons. In the realm of the individual, modern psychology provides brilliant examples of the liberating effects of a passage from the unconscious to the conscious, e.g. in the cure of the obsessional neuroses. Up to the present all commercial transactions have been the instruments of a peculiarly subtle form of bondage which was called by Marx the "fetishism of commodities". Relations, such as those of exchange in the open market between commodities, appear at first sight to be relations between things, but are, on the contrary, relations between persons, the persons who produced them and the persons who will consume them. To forget this is to be forced to assent to the various "iron laws" of political economy, which have in reality nothing inescapable about them once the personal relationship is grasped. In one of the most inspired passages he ever wrote Engels said that:

> "the seizure of the means of production by society puts an end to commodity production and hence to the domination of the product over the producer. Anarchy in social production is replaced by conscious organisation on a planned basis. The struggle for individual existence comes to an end. And at this point, in a certain sense, man finally cuts himself off from the animal world, leaves the conditions of animal existence behind him, and enters conditions which are really human. . . . It is humanity's leap from the realm of necessity into the realm of freedom."

Lastly, it must be emphasised that our present civilisation is manifestly not a state of stable equilibrium. The enormous advances in scientific knowledge and practical technique, due themselves in a large degree to the middle-class economic system of which Spencer was the representative, have made that system an anachronism. Nothing short of the absolute abolition of private ownership of resources and machines, the abolition of national sovereignties, and the government of the world by a power proceeding from the class which must abolish classes, will suit the technical situation of the twentieth century.

CHAPTER SIX

# *Beyond Atomism and Holism*

ARTHUR KOESTLER

*Hierarchies and Old Hats*

When one talks about hierarchic organisation as a fundamental principle of life, one often encounters a strong emotional resistance. For one thing, hierarchy is an ugly word, loaded with ecclesiastic and military associations, and conveys to some people a wrong impression of a rigid or authoritarian structure. (Perhaps the assonance with "hieratic", which is a quite different matter, plays a part in this confusion.) Apart from this, the term is often wrongly used to refer simply to order of rank on a linear scale or ladder (e.g., Clark Hull's "habit-family hierarchies"). But that is not at all what the term is meant to signify. Its correct symbol is not a rigid ladder but a living tree—a multilevelled, stratified, out-branching pattern of organisation, a system branching into sub-systems, which branch into sub-systems of a lower order, and so on; a structure encapsulating substructures and so on; a process activating sub-processes and so on. As Paul Weiss has declared: "The phenomenon of hierarchic structure is a real one, presented to us by the biological object, and not the fiction of a speculative mind." It is at the same time a conceptual tool, a way of thinking, an alternative to the linear chaining of events torn from their multi-dimensionally stratified contexts.

All complex structures and processes of a relatively stable character display hierarchic organisation, and this applies regardless whether we are considering inanimate systems, living organisms, social organisations, or patterns of behaviour. The linguist who thinks primarily in terms of Chomsky's hierarchic model experiences a *déjà vu* reaction towards the physiologist's intra-cellular hierarchy; and this may equally apply to Bruner's presentation of the hierarchic structure of voluntary action. In this essential respect—and in others that I shall mention—these processes in widely different fields are indeed isomorphic.

The hierarchic tree diagram may equally serve to represent the branching out of the evolution of species—the tree of life and its projection in taxonomy; it serves to represent the stepwise differentiation of tissues in embryonic development; it may serve as a structural diagram of the parts-within-parts architecture of organisms or galaxies, or as a functional schema for the analysis of instinctive behaviour by the ethologist; or of the phrase-generating machinery by the psycholinguist. It may represent the locomotor hierarchy of limbs, joints, individual muscles, and so down to fibres, fibrils and filaments; or, in reverse direction, the filtering and processing of the sensory input in its ascent from periphery to centre. It could also be regarded as a model for the subject-index of the Library of Congress, and for the organisation of knowledge in our memory-stores; lastly, as an organisational chart for government administrations, military and business organisations; and so on.

This almost universal applicability of the hierarchic model may arouse the suspicion that it is logically empty; and this may be a further factor in the resistance against it. It usually takes the form of what one may call the "so what" reaction: "all this is old hat, it is self-evident"—followed by the *non-sequitur* "and anyway, where is your evidence?" Well, hierarchy may be old hat, but I would suggest that if you handle it with some affection, it can produce quite a few lively rabbits—which can even be tested in the laboratory.

*Autonomous holons*

The evolutionary stability of sub-assemblies—organelles, organs, organ-systems—is reflected by their remarkable degree of *autonomy* or self-government. Each of them—a piece of tissue or a whole heart—is capable of functioning *in vitro* as a quasi-independent whole, even though isolated from the organism or transplanted into another organism. Each is a *sub-whole* which, towards its subordinated parts, behaves as a self-contained whole, and towards its superior controls as a dependent part. This relativity of the terms "part" and "whole" when applied to any of its sub-assemblies is a further general characteristic of hierarchies.

It is again the very obviousness of this feature which tends to make us overlook its implications. A part, as we generally use the word, means something fragmentary and incomplete, which by itself would have no legitimate existence. On the other hand, there is a tendency among holists to use the word "whole" or "Gestalt" as something complete in itself which needs no further explanation. But wholes and parts in this absolute sense do not exist anywhere, either in the domain of living organisms or of social organisations. What we find are intermediary structures on a series of levels in ascending order of complexity, each of which has two faces looking in opposite directions: the face turned towards the lower levels is that of an autonomous whole, the one turned upward that of a dependent part. I have elsewhere[1] proposed the word "holon" for these Janus-faced sub-assemblies—from the Greek *holos*—whole, with the suffix *on* (cf. neutr*on*, prot*on*) suggesting a particle or part.

The concept of the holon is meant to supply the missing link between atomism and holism, and to supplant the dualistic way of thinking in terms of "parts" and "wholes", which is so deeply engrained in our mental habits, by a multi-level, stratified approach. A hierarchically-organised whole cannot be "reduced" to its elementary parts; but it can be "dissected" into its constituent branches of holons, represented by the nodes of the tree-diagram, while the lines connecting the holons stand for channels of communication, control or transportation, as the case may be.

### *Fixed rules and flexible strategies*

*The term holon may be applied to any stable sub-whole in an organismic, cognitive, or social/hierarchy which displays rule-governed behaviour and/or structural Gestalt constancy.* Thus biological holons are self-regulating "open systems" (von Bertalanffy 1952) governed by a set of fixed rules which account for the holon's coherence, stability and its specific pattern of structure and function. This set of rules we may call *the canon of the holon.*[2] The canon determines the fixed, invariant aspect of the open system in its steady state (*Fliessgleichgewicht*—dynamic equilibrium); it defines its pattern and structure. In other types of hierarchies, the canon represents the codes of conduct of social holons (family, tribe,

[1] *The Ghost in the Machine* (1967).
[2] cf. the "organizing relations" or "laws of organization" of earlier writers on hierarchic organisation (e.g. Woodger (1929), Needham (1941)), and the "system-conditions" in General System Theory.

nation, etc.); it incorporates the "rules of the game" of instinctive rituals or acquired skills (behavioural holons); the rules of enunciation, grammar and syntax in the language hierarchy; Piaget's "schemes" in cognitive hierarchies, and so on. *The canon represents the constraints imposed on any role-governed process or behaviour*. But these constraints do not exhaust the system's degrees of freedom; they leave room for more or less *flexible strategies*, guided by the contingencies in the holon's local environment.

It is essential at this point to make a sharp, categorical distinction between the fixed, invariant canon of the system and its flexible (plastic, variable) strategies. A few examples will illustrate the validity of this distinction. In *ontogeny*, the apex of the hierarchy is the zygote, and the holons at successive levels represent successive stages in the development of tissues. Each step in differentiation and specialisation imposes further constraints on the genetic potential of the tissue, but at each step it retains sufficient developmental flexibility to follow this or that evolutionary pathway, within the range of its competence, guided by the contingencies of the cell's environment—Waddington's "strategy of the genes". Turning from embryonic development to the *instinctive activities* of the mature animal, we find that spiders spin webs, birds build nests according to invariant species-specific canons, but again using flexible strategies, guided by the lie of the land: the spider may suspend its web from three, four or more points of attachment, but the result will always be a regular polygon. In *acquired skills* like chess, the rules of the game define the permissible moves, but the strategic choice of the actual move depends on the environment—the distribution of the chessmen on the board. In *symbolic operations*, the holons are rule-governed cognitive structures variously called "frames of reference", "universes of discourse", "algorithms", etc., each with its specific "grammar" or canon; and the strategies increase in complexity on higher levels of each hierarchy. It seems that life in all its manifestations, from morphogenesis to symbolic thought, is governed by rules of the game which lend it order and stability but also allow for flexibility; and that these rules, whether innate or acquired, are represented in coded form on various levels of the hierarchy, from the genetic code to the structures in the nervous system responsible for symbolic thought.

### *Triggers and Scanners*

Let me discuss briefly some specific characteristics of what one might loosely call *output hierarchies*, regardless whether the "output" is a baby, or a sentence spoken in English. However much their products differ, all output hierarchies seem to have a classic mode of operation, based on the trigger-releaser principle, where an implicit coded signal which may be relatively simple, releases complex pre-set mechanisms.

Let me again run through a few examples. In *phylogeny*, Waddington and others have convincingly shown that a single favourable gene-mutation can act as a trigger to release a kind of chain-reaction which affects a whole organ in a harmonious way. In *ontogeny*, the prick of a fine platinum needle on the unfertilised egg of a frog or sheep triggers off parthenogenesis. The genes act as chemical triggers, catalysing reactions. The implicit four-letter alphabet of the DNA chain is spelled out into the explicit, twenty-letter alphabet of amino acids; the inducers or evocators, including Spemann's "general organiser", again turn out to be relatively simple chemicals which need not even be species-specific to activate the genetic potentials of the tissue. In *instinct behaviour*, we have releasers of a very simple kind—the red belly of the stickleback, the spot under the herring-gull's beak, which trigger off the appropriate behaviour. In the performance of *acquired skills* you have the same process of stepwise filling in the details of implicit commands issued from the apex of the hierarchy, such as "strike a match and light this cigarette" or "sing your name", or "use your phrase-generating machine" to transform an unverbalised image into innervations of the vocal chords.

The point to emphasise is that this spelling-out process, from intent to execution, cannot be described in terms of a linear chain of S-R units, only as a series of discrete steps from one Open Sesame, activated by a combination lock, to the next. The activated holon whether it is a government department or a living kidney, has its own canon which determines the pattern of its activity. Thus the signal from higher quarters does not have to specify what the holon is expected to do; the signal merely has to trigger the holon into action by a coded message. Once thrown into action the holon will spell out the implicit command in explicit form by activating its sub-units in the appropriate strategic order, guided by feedbacks and feed-forwards from its environment. Generally speaking, *the holon is a system of relations which is represented on the next higher level as a unit, that is, a relatum.*

If we turn now to the *input hierarchies* of perception, the operations proceed, of course, in the reverse direction, from the peripheral twigs of the tree towards its apex; and instead of trigger-releasers we have the opposite type of mechanisms: a series of filters, scanners or classifiers through which the input traffic must pass in its ascent from periphery to cortex. First you have lateral inhibition, habituation and presumably some efferent control of receptors. On the higher levels are the mechanisms responsible for the visual and acoustic constancy phenomena, the scanning and filtering devices which account for the recognition of patterns in space and time, and enable us to abstract universals and discard particulars. The colloquial complaint: "I have a memory like a sieve" may be derived from an intuitive grasp of these filtering devices that operate first all along the input channels, then along the storage channels.

How do we pick out a single instrument in a symphony? The whole medley of sounds arriving at the ear-drum is scrambled into a linear pressure-wave with a single variable. To reconstruct the timbre of an instrument, to identify harmonies and melodies, to appreciate phrasing, style and mood, we have to abstract patterns in time as we abstract visual patterns in space. But how does the nervous system do it? If one looks at a gramophone record with a magnifying glass, one is tempted to ask the naïve question why the nervous system does not produce engrams by this simple method of coding, instead of being so complicated. The answer is, of course, that a linear engram of this kind would be completely useless for the purpose of analysing, matching and recognising input patterns.

In motor hierarchies, an implicit intention or generalised command is particularised, spelled out, step by step, in its descent to the periphery. In perceptual hierarchies, we have the opposite process. The peripheral input is more and more de-particularised, stripped of irrelevancies during its ascent to the centre. The *output hierarchy concretises, the input hierarchy abstracts.* The former operates by means of triggering devices, the latter by means of filtering or scanning devices. When I intend to write the letter R, a trigger activates a functional holon, an automatic pattern of muscle contractions, which produces the letter R in my own particular handwriting. When I read, a scanning device in my visual cortex identifies the letter R regardless of the particular hand that wrote it. Triggers release complex outputs by means of a simple coded signal. Scanners function the opposite way: they convert complex inputs into simple coded signals.

*Arborisation and Reticulation*

I have used the term "interlocking" or "interlacing" hierarchies. Of course hierarchies do not operate in a vacuum. This truism regarding the interdependence of processes in an organism is probably the main causes of confusion which obscured from view its hierarchic structure. It is as if the sight of the foliage of the entwined branches in a forest made us forget that the branches originate in separate trees. The trees are vertical structures. The meeting points of branches from neighbouring trees form horizontal networks at several levels. Without the trees there could be no entwining, and no network. Without the networks, each tree would be isolated, and there would be no integration of functions. Arborisation and reticulation seem to be complementary principles in the architecture of organisms. In symbolic universes of discourse arborisation is reflected in the "vertical" denotation (definition) of concepts, reticulation in their "horizontal" connotations in associative networks. This calls to mind Hyden's proposal that the same neuron, or population of neurons, may be a member of several functional "clubs".

*Hierarchic order and Feedback Control*

The most obvious example of interlocking hierarchies is the sensory-motor system. The sensory hierarchy processes information and transmits it in a steady upward flow, some of which reaches the conscious ego at the apex; the ego makes decisions which are spelled out by the downward stream of impulses in the motor hierarchy. But the apex is not the only point of contact between the two systems; they are connected by entwining networks on various lower levels. The network on the lowest level consists of reflexes like the patellary. They are short-cuts between the ascending and descending flow, like loops connecting opposite traffic streams on a motor highway. On the next higher level are the networks of sensory-motor skills and habits, such as touch-typing or driving a car, which do not require the attention of the highest centres—unless some disturbance throws them out of gear. But let a little dog amble across the icy road in front of the driver, and he will have to make a "top level" decision whether to slam down the brake, risking the safety of his passengers, or run over the dog. It is at this level, when the pros and cons are precariously balanced, that the subjective experience of free choice and moral responsibility arises.

But the ordinary routines of existence do not require such

moral decisions, and not even much conscious attention. They operate by means of feedback loops, and loops-within-loops, which form the multi-levelled, reticulate networks between the input and output hierarchies. So long as all goes well and no dog crosses the road, the strategy of riding a bicycle or driving a car can be left to the automatic pilot in the nervous system—the cybernetic helmsman. But one must beware of using the principle of feedback control as a magic formula. The concept of feedback without the concept of hierarchic order is like the grin without the cat. All skilled routines follow a preset pattern according to certain rules of the game. These are fixed, but permit constant adjustments to variable environmental conditions. *Feedback can only operate within the limits set by the rules*—by the canon of the skill. The part which feedback plays is to report back on every step in the progress of the operation, whether it is over-shooting or falling short of the mark, how to keep it on an even keel, when to intensify the pace and when to stop. But it cannot alter the intrinsic pattern of the skill. To quote Paul Weiss at the Hixon Symposium: "The structure of the input does not produce the structure of the output, but merely modifies intrinsic nervous activities, which have a structural organization of their own." One of the vital differences between the S-R and SOHO concepts is that according to the former, the environment determines behaviour, whereas according to the latter, feedback from the environment merely guides or corrects or stabilises pre-existing patterns of behaviour.

Moreover, the cross-traffic between the sensory and motor hierarchies works both ways. The input guides the output and keeps it on an even keel; but motor activity in its turn guides perception. The eye must scan; its motions, large and small—drift flicker, tremor—are indispensable to vision; an image stabilised on the retina disintegrates into darkness. Similarly with audition: if you try to recall a tune, what do you do? You hum it. Stimuli and responses have been swallowed up by feedback loops within loops, along which impulses run in circles like kittens chasing their tails.

*A Hierarchy of Environments*

Let us carry this inquiry into the meaning of current terminology a step further, and ask just what the convenient word "environment" is meant to signify. When I am driving my car, the environment in contact with my right foot is the accelerator pedal, its elastic resistance to pressure provides a tactile feedback which helps keeping the speed of the car steady. The same applies to the "feel" of the wheel under my hands. But my eyes encompass a much larger environment than my feet and hands; they determine the overall strategy of driving. The hierarchically organised creature that I am is in fact functioning in a hierarchy of environments, guided by a hierarchy of feedbacks.

One advantage of this operational interpretation is that the hierarchy of environments can be extended indefinitely. When the chess-player stares at the board in front of him, trying to visualise various situations three moves ahead, he is guided by feedbacks from imagined environments. Most of our thinking, planning and creating operates in such imaginary environments. But—to quote Bartlett—"all our preceptions are inferential constructs", coloured by imagination, and so the difference is merely one of degrees. The hierarchy is open-ended at the top.

*Regulation channels*

When the centipede was asked in which order he moved his hundred legs, he became paralysed and starved to death because he had never thought of it before, and had left his legs to look after themselves. When an intent is formed at the apex of the hierarchy, such as signing a letter, it does not activate individual motor units, but triggers off patterns of impulses which activate sub-patterns and so on. But this can only be done one step at a time: the higher centres do not normally have dealings with lowly ones, and vice versa. Brigadiers do not concentrate their attention on individual soldiers—if they did, the whole operation would go haywire. Commands must be transmitted through "regulation channels".

This statement looks trivial, but ignoring it carries heavy penalties of a theoretical or practical order. Attempting to short-circuit intermediary levels of the hierarchy by focusing conscious attention on physiological processes which otherwise function automatically, usually ends in the centipede's predicament, reflected in symptoms that range from impotence and frigidity to constipation and spastic colons.

As for theory, the S-R psychologist's attempt to short-circuit hierarchic levels by vague references to "intervening variables" is a face-saving manoeuvre to sweep all the essential problems of complex human behaviour, including language, under the laboratory carpet.

The tendency towards the progressive mechanisation of skills has its positive side: it conforms to the principle of parsimony. If I could not hit the keys of the typewriter "automatically" I could not attend to meaning. On the negative side, mechanisation, like rigor mortis, affects first the extremities—the lower subordinate branches of the hierarchy, but it also tends to spread upward. If a skill is practised in the same unvarying conditions, following the same unvarying course, it tends to degenerate into stereotyped routine and its degrees of freedom freeze up. Monotony accelerates enslavement to habit; and if mechanisation spreads to the apex of the hierarchy, the result is the rigid pedant, Bergson's *homme automatie*. As von Bertalanffy says, "organisms *are not* machines, but they can to a certain extent *become* machines, congeal into machines".

Vice versa, a variable environment demands flexible behaviour and reverses the trend towards mechanisation. However, the challenge of the environment may exceed a critical limit where it can no longer be met by customary routines, however flexible—because the traditional "rules of the game" are no longer adequate to cope with the situation. Then a crisis arises. The outcome is either a breakdown of behaviour—or alternatively the emergence of new forms of behaviour, of original solutions. They have been observed throughout the animal kingdom, from insects onward, through rats to chimpanzees, and point to the existence of unsuspected potentials in the living organism, which are inhibited or dormant in the normal routines of existence, and only make their appearance in exceptional circumstances. They foreshadow the phenomena of human creativity which must remain incomprehensible to the S-R theorist, but appear in a new light when approached from the hierarchic point of view.

### *Self-assertion and Integration*

The holons which constitute an organismic or social hierarchy are Janus-faced entities: facing upward, towards the apex, they function as dependent parts of a larger whole; facing downward, as autonomous wholes in their own right. "Autonomy" in this context means that organelles, cells, muscles, neurons, organs, all have their intrinsic rhythm and pattern, often manifested spontaneously without external stimulation, and that they tend to persist in and assert their characteristic pattern of activity. This *self-assertive tendency* is a fundamental and universal characteristic of holons, manifested on every level of every type of hierarchy: in the regulative properties of the morphogenetic field, defying transplantation and experimental mutilation; in the stubbornness of instinct rituals, acquired habits, tribal traditions and social customs; and even in a person's handwriting, which he can modify but not sufficiently to fool the expert. Without this self-assertive tendency of their parts, organisms and societies would lose their articulation and stability.

The opposite aspect of the holon is its *integrative tendency* to function as an integral part of an existing or evolving larger whole. Its manifestations are equally ubiquitous, from the "docility" of the embryonic tissues, through the symbiosis of organelles in the cell, to the various forms of cohesive bonds, from flock to insect state and human tribe.

If we turn from organismic to *social hierarchies*, we again find that under normal conditions the holons (clans, tribes, nations, social classes, professional groups) live in a kind of dynamic equilibrium with their natural and social environment. However, under conditions of stress, when tensions exceed a critical limit, some social holon may get over-excited and tend to assert itself to the detriment of the whole, just like an over-excited organ. It should be noted that the canon which defines the identity and lends coherence to social holons (its laws, language, traditions, rules of conduct, systems of belief) represents not merely negative constraints imposed on its actions, but also positive precepts, maxims and moral imperatives.

The single individual constitutes the apex of the organismic hierarchy, and at the same time the lowest unit of the social hierarchy. Looking inward, he sees himself as a self-contained, unique whole; looking outward as a dependent part. No man is an island, he is a holon. His *self-assertive* tendency is the dynamic manifestation of his unique wholeness as an individual; his *integrative* tendency expresses his dependence on the larger whole to which he belongs, his partners. Under normal conditions, the two opposite tendencies are more or less evenly balanced. Under conditions of stress, the equilibrium is upset, as manifested in emotional behaviour. The emotions derived from the self-assertive tendencies are of the well-known aggressive-defensive, hunger, rage and fear type, including the possessive component of sex. The emotions derived from the integrative tendency have been largely neglected by contemporary psychology; one may call them the self-transcending or participatory type of emotions. They arise out of the human holon's need to be an integral part of some larger whole—which may be a social group, a personal bond, a belief-system, Nature or the *anima mundi*. The psychological processes through which this category of emotions operates are variously referred to as projection, identification, empathy, hypnotic rapport, devotion, love. It is one of the ironies of the human condition that both its glory and its predicament seem to derive not from the self-assertive but from the integrative potentials of the species. The glories of art and science, and the holocausts of history caused by misguided devotion, are both nurtured by the self-transcending emotions.

CHAPTER SEVEN

# *Nature, Life and Mind*

OWEN ST. JOHN

It is a fault in some distinguished minds to imagine that they are necessarily as competent in philosophy as they are in their own special field. In the 1920's we had an example in the relation of physics to philosophy. Sir Arthur Eddington, mathematician and astronomer, and Sir James Jeans, also an astronomer, sought to persuade us that science had completely disintegrated the physical world into the abstractions of contemporary physics,[1] Jeans went further and dissolved physics into mathematics and therefore into the mental.[2] Their books were read, reviewed and discussed on a wide scale; but after a burst of public interest and even excitement, their theories were critically demolished[3] and today they are almost completely forgotten.

This happens again and again. Monod, authoritative and convincing in the sphere of molecular biology proclaims his full acceptance of the philosophical views of his brilliant compatriot of 300 years ago—René Descartes (1596–1650) and then involves himself in the contradictions of a discredited empiricism. The result is total confusion.

The ideas of Descartes exerted an immense influence in his time and beyond it, but they belong to a particular juncture—the birth of modern astronomy, the Newtonian philosophy, and the break-up of the medieval synthesis; but the further discoveries in chemistry and biology, the theory of evolution, and the replacement of rationalism as a philosophy by the development of British empiricism (Locke, Berkeley, Hume) had the result that every single article in the Cartesian

[1] Eddington, *The Nature of the Physical World.*
[2] Jeans, *The Mysterious Universe.*
[3] Stebbing, *Philosophy and the Physicists.*

philosophy was questioned. The result is an appalling muddle in Monod's thought. Monod has himself complained of "able and distinguished scientists who have not applied their scientific objectivity to the causes they support to the extent they would in their professional work, yet are using their great prestige, perhaps as Nobel Prize winners, to give assurance to the general public that they have judged these issues on the basis of their scientific authority".[4] And that is just what has gone wrong in Monod's very able book *Chance and Necessity*. The scientific work is convincing and gives a useful summary of the theories of molecular biology which represent a milestone in the scientific discovery. But in its basic Cartesian reductionism Monod's reasoning is sadly defective, and quite unable to sustain either the evolutionary theories or the social and ethical principles which form the themes of the later chapters.

A dead and mechanical world of matter, as conceived by Cartesian physics, cannot conceivably produce life by doing the only thing which it has the power to do, namely, redistributing itself in space.

> The conception of vital process as distinct from mechanical or chemical change has come to stay, and has revolutionised our conception of nature.[5]

Above all, it is impossible to describe one and the same thing in the same breath as a machine and as developing or evolving. A machine is essentially a finished product; the only kind of change which it can produce in itself is breaking down or wearing out. But living organisms are not passive but basically active and developing systems. The continuous building up of components from simplest materials is inherent in living things, and above all, and in complete opposition to the machine, the organism is maintaining and increasing its energy while every physical system is only using its energy up.

Cartesianism thus becomes a falsification of experience from the first; and the modern Cartesian, in describing the world of experience as bits of matter moved by mechanical law and nothing more, is not reasoning scientifically, in terms of observable data, he is arguing for a metaphysics.

Nor can Popper be right in endorsing their efforts as com-

[4] BBC interview, July 1970.
[5] Collingwood, *The Idea of Nature*.

mendable because, for example, in seeking to reduce all experience to matter in motion they revealed the physical conditions of sight and sound. This was not the motive of the scientists who discovered the cause of light to be undulatory or particulate, and the cause of sound to be vibrations of a particular wavelength. Pythagoras was not trying to eliminate music when he explained musical notes mathematically, nor was Huygens trying to get rid of the experience of light and colour. It is only the metaphysician who aims at this; the scientist, as a scientist seeks for *the physical correlate* and never thinks in terms of *reduction* in the Cartesian sense. The moment he does so he ceases to be a scientist, and becomes a metaphysician.

Exactly the same reasoning demands the recognition of the objectivity of life and mind in spite of the fact that they are necessarily correlated with and dependent upon chemical and physical processes. But the Cartesian fear of life and mind overrides all considerations of logic and common sense for the metaphysician who reduces both to mechanism.

It is strange that Monod appears to believe that his Cartesian views on objectivity and certainty are identical with the philosophical views of Karl Popper who has spent his long life in an exhaustive refutation of them. When Monod declares his "complete adherence to his views", all one can say is that he has totally failed to understand them.

In considering these questions as in most of the problems of perception, induction and scientific reasoning, the biologist who has not had a philosophical training, particularly if his philosophical clock stopped ticking at 1670 and hasn't moved since, invariably goes astray; and becomes involved in needless and unescapable complications.

> Descartes and Monod believe that we obtain knowledge by the direct grasp of the mathematical essence of things. On the contrary, argues Popper, we never do this; we cannot get beyond imperfect and always corrigible hypotheses.
>
> Descartes believes that *truth is manifest*, Popper has written whole essays to show that this is exactly what it is not and to rebut what he calls "the optimistic epistemology of Descartes". The truth is not there for everyone to see if they will simply be objective in their judgments. On the contrary it can never be found except in our distorted and incomplete versions of it.

> Monod believes that all the laws of nature, including those of biology and neurology, which cover all the facts of life and mind, follow from one basic mechanical and rational system. Popper points out that all such laws are contingent and refutable, none of them have the necessity that belongs only to the empty and purely formal concepts of logic and mathematics. We have no ultimate explanation and the more we learn about theories, or the laws of nature, the less do they appear to be ultimate, irreducible and manifest.

There is a further point of some importance. Why is the method operated on the assumption of the ultimate facts being particulate, that a thing's *parts* are ultimate and more real than the thing itself? This is a pure assumption. It works for the gas laws; but is that a good reason for insisting on applying it *everywhere*, even when it is plainly nonsense? Clearly the extrapolation of such a model, or indeed of any model concerned to classify thought *in particular cases or situations*, to the whole of reality, is logically absurd. In arguing thus we are passing from science to metaphysics, and very bad metaphysics at that—a metaphysical demand that science must explain all the phenomena of nature, including man, morals, culture and art in terms of one hypothesis of maximum simplicity and impersonality. But we can never extrapolate from a deliberately restricted sphere to all possible spheres, to all aspects and levels of existence. Scientific thinking based on experience allows only conditional explanations within stated limits. We can never arrive in science at an unconditional generalisation that *everything, under all possible conditions*, everything that is, or will be, or has been, is of such and such a nature and behaves in such and such a way. This obviously transcends all possible experience. Unconditional statements about the universe do not conform to the scientific pattern of thinking.

The conclusion from a particulate and one level model also proves unacceptable and contrary to the evidence of experience. It would follow: (*a*) that values are impossible, as Monod admits, for particulate facts lose all the contextual significance required for evaluation; (*b*) that all wholes become aggregates not organisations with their own characteristics and laws, merely a crowd of random motions governed by statistical laws; (*c*) that real change, development, and the emergence of novelty is impossible.

Monod himself bears witness to the cogency of such criticisms by demonstrating point by point the inadequacy of his philosophy to account for the facts which his reductionism denies but which his own concern for objectivity compels him to admit.

*The Origin of Life*

The coming together of the necessary components and external physical conditions, including the requisite radiations from outer space, created a unique set of circumstances in which, by a series of steps, the first macro-molecules appeared; then their capacity to replicate; after that their association in the first living cell. This theory, in its several forms, was first suggested by the Russian Oparin in 1924, and independently by J. B. S. Haldane in 1929. Since then it has been vigorously discussed and amended and has for some time been generally accepted.[6]

During the whole of this first and supremely important stage in natural development the element of chance is generally recognised as playing a necessary part. But whether it is sufficient would appear to be questioned by Monod, though he still insists on chance and nothing else, when he admits the *potentiality* of life and all subsequent evolutionary achievements in the first elementary particles. More explicitly, Whitehead speaks of: "The notion of creative activity belonging to the very essence of each occasion. It is the process of eliciting into actual being factors in the universe which antecedently to that process exist only in the mode of unrealised potentialities."[7] This suggests that something more is required than the necessary physical conditions—which are not in themselves sufficient to achieve the immensely significant step to life and all its portends. That something is not an intrusion from without or a life-force within, but something intrinsic to the material association itself. What that will be becomes plainer when we turn to the next stage in evolution.

*The Progressive Diversity of Life*

Monod explains how the genetic variations occurring by change secure by selection a better adaptation to environmental demands that creates new and more advanced forms. But he points out that there

[6] See S. W. Fox, *The Origin of Prebiological Systems* (1965), and J. D. Bernal's *The Origin of Life* (1967). Monod makes use, correctly, of these generally accepted theories. They are not his own.

[7] Whitehead, *Modes of Thought*.

must be something more than that because a very large number of plants and animals adapt very successfully at a low level of evolutionary development and persist over hundreds of millions of years in exactly the same environment in which immense advances have been made by other organisms. We may mention algae, mosses and ferns, and, of course, an enormous range of invertebrate animals: the little sea-shell *Lingula* has hardly changed from its ancestor in the fossil strata of 400 million years ago, and an oyster of 200 million years or more in the past would look perfectly familiar if served in a restaurant today. Even more remarkable are the silica-secreting protozoans or Radiolaria which have existed since the pre-Cambrian rocks of 500 million years ago.

These are but a few indications of the problem which is emerging. There appear not only adaptation but first, progressive development, and then non-adaptive variations—a multitude of types within the same area of environmental requirements, as among groups of flowers, and finally the adaptive variation resulting from animals seeking new environments and then adapting themselves to it—land animals taking to the sea and becoming seals and whales, squirrels going up the trees, moles going below ground. Both the *progressive* character of evolution[8] and adaptation, not to the environment in which the animal's ancestor is found, but to one that he chooses are eloquently described by Monod himself.

> "Because a primitive fish 'chose' to do some exploring on land, where it could however only move about by clumsy hops, this fish thereby created, as a consequence of a change in behaviour, the selective pressure which was to engender the powerful limbs of the quadrupeds,"

and also, of course, the lungs which enabled them to breathe.

Professor Waddington has for many years been pointing out how this choice of a new environment results in a process of genetic assimilation, that is to say the animal first adapts itself as best it may to the new circumstances, as when we increase the number of red blood corpuscles if we go and live at a great height for a number of years.

[8] Julian Huxley in his *Evolution, the Modern Synthesis* has a useful discussion on evolutionary progress which he defines as increasing independence of environmental demands, e.g., a wide range of temperatures, ability to breath in air, increased complexity of organisation; improved sense organs and brain; and improvements which, unlike specialisation, permit further development.

This acquired character is eventually inherited, but not in the Lamarckism fashion but by means that are quite explicable by ordinary genetic laws.[9] Monod also shows how "the initial choice of a certain kind of behaviour sets the species on the road to a continuous perfecting of the structures and performances which support his behaviour".[10]

This is possible in living organisms but not in machines. Machines don't "choose" to become something different. A horse-drawn carriage does not "choose" to become a motor-car. Machines do not evolve by themselves. The conception of development is fatal to reductive materialism. When Monod sees his fish as "going exploring on land", as a matter of "choice" he has gone entirely beyond his materialism. It is clear that Monod realises this. He explains convincingly how evolution proceeds by gradual but definite transitional steps through a successive series of new types of order, with a gradual rise to dominance of biological laws. This is a creative advance from one form of order or set of laws to another on a higher level.

But Monod has now been precipitated from the realm of mechanical interactions of particles into the formerly rejected world of life and mind—a complete *volte face*. He gives us, as a matter of fact, a convincing demonstration of the theory of integrative levels and the rising hierarchical series that he summarily rejected in his chapter on *Vitalisms and Animisms*.

The essence of the evolutionary process is that first there exist entities with a structure and character of their own, and then they are arranged in a new pattern under particular conditions, and a new order of qualities appears and a new law system; each stage of this process being marked by the emergence of a new and more adequate type of individuality embracing and transcending now as parts of itself the previously existing wholes or organs which made it up.[11]

Monod, after rebuking the biologists who take this position as animists, produced in his chapter on *Evolution* an admirable and convincing account of the emergence of living and thinking organisms, in flat contradiction to what he has just so strenuously affirmed. It is strange that most of the reviewers and those who have engaged in public controversy with Monod have failed to notice this hiatus.

In the excellent pages he devotes to this theme he clearly

[9] *Nature* (1942). *The Strategy of the Genes. Evolutionary Adaptation* in "Evolution after Darwin", and again in *Nature* (1959).
[10] Monod, *Chance and Necessity*.
[11] See Koestler, *Beyond Atomism and Holism*, Chapter 6.

recognises the progressive character of the series of forms, in spite of some regressions (notably in parasites) and some unchanging species. He is eloquent on the qualitative differences that mechanism denies. Attributing this progress to chance, nevertheless he does not question the novelty and the higher qualities of the evolved forms. Many biologists who have no use for vitalism or any other form of dualism question the "pure chance" explanation of this process. It is difficult, indeed it seems highly improbable, that pure chance operating with physically limited entities in mechanical interaction could, by no matter how many billions of throws of the dice, bring into existence the complex structures and remarkable qualities of such animals as the bee or the humming bird and eventually man himself. It has been asserted that if a sufficient number of chance events are allowed for, the whole of Shakespeare's *Hamlet* would one day appear. Or, as the well-known limerick says:

> There once was a brainy baboon
> Who always breathed down a bassoon,
> For he said "It appears
> In billions of years
> I shall certainly hit on a tune."

The point is that variation and survival might conceivably secure adaptation, a state of equilibrium, such as we find in the well-adapted molluscs which have survived for so long. However we are not thinking of survival but of improvement, or progress; and here it must be remembered, Monod is not, as some rather foolish controversialists do, arguing that there is no reason to regard the cockroach as any higher than the mammal. Monod asserts, and strongly argues for, the emergence of new and higher realms of being. We have to explain the fact of uniqueness, of qualitative progress. We cannot refuse to accept it because of an *a priori* commitment to the dogma of "nothing but", nor can we continue to hold our reductionist position and at the same time accept the facts which contradict it—the position that Monod appears to take up.

It is, of course, when he comes to man and his mind that we get the clearest statement of the transcendance of mechanism. Man, for Monod, is something far beyond the merely conditioned ratomorphic man of the behaviourists, though this and the limitation of human responses to reflexes and instincts, is the necessary conclusion of the mechanistic materialist. On the contrary he gives us an excellent account of the nature and unique quality of reason, he shows how language arises and that it is not the same thing as the signal sounds that we find in animal communication. We are now, to use his own words in "the kingdom of culture, of ideas, of knowledge—a unique event in the biosphere". This puts Monod in the ranks of the organicists and comes very close to Teilhard's account of man in *The Phenomenon of Man*. As Dr. John Lewis explains:[12]

> Teilhard called his book *The Phenomenon of Man* because he describes man's origin and development in strictly empirical terms, without introducing into his objective account any mystical or transcendental evolutionary principle. As he said, "I have not tried to discover a system of ontological and causal relations, but only an experimental explanation." This he explains in his preface, and repeats again and again in the course of his exposition. The origin of life is dealt with in terms of macromolecules and physical conditions, evolution in terms of variations and selection, the emergence of man as the result of the anatomical changes in hand and foot and skull and the development of the brain. Then he adds in a footnote that the theologian or philosopher may seek to supplement the physical series as described with a metaphysical explanation beyond the phenomena; but that is something quite distinct from his own purpose in the empirical account of the phenomenon of man. The philosopher, of course, is as much at liberty to do this as a mathematical philosopher to say that beyond the limits of pure mathematics, and independent of its theorems, he hypothecates God, the pure mathematician, as its creator (as did the astronomer Sir James Jeans). We may disagree, but that does not detract in the slightest from the validity of his mathematics or astronomy.

Monod's book falls into two inconsistent halves. If we take the first half seriously and are convinced by it, we reject the theory of integrative levels and emergent evolution and are committed to the reductionism which denies biological progress and finds a complete explanation of life and mind in the terms of physics and chemistry. Monod's materialism makes nonsense of his evolutionism and his

[12] *The Teilhard Review*, February, 1973.

humanism. If these are at all costs to be saved, if he really believes them, as they are so lucidly set forth in the second half of the book, then all this makes nonsense of his reductionism. How does he escape from this dilemma? It can only be by an irrational leap of faith into the realm of values, the realm of mind and knowledge. The limitations of the Cartesian philosophy, to which Monod is dedicated, force him into the existentialist choice of Jean Paul Sartre. His kingdom of reason and value is based on the arbitrary postulates, first of scientific reason, then of all the values necessary for the realm of humanism.

*The Limitations of Molecular Biology*

Few of his readers would feel competent to question or even to discuss the exposition of molecular biology which forms the ground of Monod's case. But we must recognise that molecular biology is not the whole of reality but an abstracted aspect. When it is forced to play the sole part of evolutionary agent and progressive change, when it is declared to have explained in purely mechanical terms the *choosing* animal and the thinking man, we cannot but become acutely aware that the molecular biologist has gone beyond the limits of his province of inquiry.

Our doubts are supported by many who are themselves conversant with the technical problems, as most of us are not. It is from molecular biologists that criticism now comes. Professor Barry Commoner argues that it cannot be said that the precise replication of DNA is due to the inherent chemical capabilities of the molecule. Many features of inheritance are incompatible with the operations of the Watson-Crick system.[13]

Professor Waddington has his own line of criticism and Dr. Robin Monro, who has worked with Crick in Cambridge is by no means satisfied with Monod's position.[14] This means that it is not to be assumed that the highly technical chapters in this book must receive our unqualified acceptance.

*Existential Ethics*

In the second half it is now clear that we are situated in the realm of

[13] See Commoner's papers in *Science* (1961), also his *Horizons in Biochemistry* (1967), etc. Professor Paul Weiss regards the theory of "a bag of molecular units milling around in thermal agitation" creating the living cell, as beyond credibility. That it should produce the whole panorama of animal and plant life and the whole scene of human culture and history simply cannot be believed.

[14] See Chapter 9.

mind and values. Evolution has carried us into a mind directed order in which men use symbolic language dealing with general ideas opening the way for man to

> another evolution, creator of a new kingdom: that of culture of ideas, of knowledge. This was a unique event ... one of those crucial choices which decide the future of the species.[15]

We are now in a world of preferences, choices, creative possibilities. Preference implies values, but how have values appeared in a world of pure molecular interactions? Monod's reply is, that since they cannot be derived from this source and "science is the enemy of values" they must be postulated. We are therefore invited to choose our ethical postulates: first, the ethical principle of scientific objectivity, itself a moral choice. This establishes the rational order of scientific thinking which excludes everything but the Cartesian world of molecular interactions based on the laws of physics. But, that of course, is not enough. We need a further set of postulates. In the *Controversy* programme at the Royal Institution, Monod stated that he was

> aware that many other choices will have to be made, the postulates necessary to constitute a system of values compatible with the twentieth century. These will be a system of normative choices.

It is hardly surprising that having reduced the richness of our world to one component and one set of physical laws, Monod then finding himself bereft of all values, cannot but join the ranks of the empiricist philosophers and support them in their rejection of "the naturalistic fallacy". This so-called "fallacy" is itself the disastrous consequence of a real fallacy which the philosopher Whitehead calls "the fallacy of misplaced concreteness": the habit of abstracting a part and ascribing to it the sort of reality that belongs to the whole. In this case the measureable and *physically* observable is taken to be the only reality objectively speaking, so that values become purely subjective. This familiar argument is wearing very thin.[16] Professor Bernard Williams[17] has pointed out that many situations involve the inseparable unity of a judgment of fact and a judgment of value, so that the whole

[15] Monod, *Chance and Necessity*, p. 123.
[16] See W. K. Frankena's article in Mind (1939); reprinted in Sellars and Hospers, *Readings in Ethical Theory*, and see also Abraham Edel's *Ethical Judgment*.
[17] In *Modern British Philosophy* (ed. Magee).

situation as experienced is a fact possessing in its very nature as that fact a definite value. *Being poisonous* is strictly factual and also negatively valued. If as a matter of *fact* a man owes money, the very statement implies that he *ought* to repay it. A treacherous deed, a sentimental novel, a promissory note, cannot be chopped up, says Williams, into simple *ought* and *is*. Then take such statements as "It's his job to look after his passengers". Here you can't separate the obligation from the fact without disintegrating the whole system of social relationships.

This separation of *fact* and *value* was first proclaimed by Hume, and again in our time by G. E. Moore, and now most eloquently by Jacques Monod:

> "It is perfectly true that science attacks values. . . ." "The postulate of objectivity forbids any confusion of value judgments with judgments arrived at through knowledge". "Values, duties, rights, prohibitions . . ." "Knowledge in itself is exclusive of value judgment, whereas ethics, in essence non-objective is for ever barred from the sphere of knowledge. . . ." "If he accepts this message in its full significance, man must at last wake out of his millenary dream and discover his total solitude, his fundamental isolation. He must realise that he lives on the boundary of an alien world, a world that is deaf to his music, and as indifferent to his hopes as it is to his suffering or his crimes."[18]

Now, of course, it is certainly the case that if you abstract *one* single measureable aspect of complex reality and then declare that nothing else has any objective reality, you will certainly find no objective ground for value. As Leibnitz said of Hume's failure to find the knowing mind. "A man goes out of his house, looks in at the window, and is surprised to find that the room is empty." The surveyor instructed to measure up a building tells us that in his very fundamental investigation, he has discovered no design, no purpose and no beauty. But what he has been instructed to leave out of account cannot be expected to be described in that account.

As a result of this extrusion of everything but the physical from the real world all moral judgments and values are suspended in a vacuum, and cannot but degenerate into subjective likes, dislikes and

[18] *Chance and Necessity*, pp. 160, 162.

even whims. As Moore argued there can be no dispute over ethical questions except in terms of tastes which the disputants happen to share. If they have different tastes discussion must cease.

> "If, when one man says, 'this action is right', and another answers, 'No, it is not right', each of them is always merely making an assertion about his own feelings, it plainly follows that there is never really any difference of opinion between them: the one of them is never really contradicting what the other is asserting. They are no more contradicting one another than if when one had said, 'I like sugar', the other had answered, 'I don't like sugar. . . .' It follows, therefore that no two men can ever differ in opinion as to whether an action is right or wrong."[19]

Moses blew off his emotions about murder by saying "thou shalt not kill", and if a killer from Auschwitz happens to feel differently, *de gustibus non disputandum.*

It is frequently assumed that to turn from reason to instinct is necessarily to find a new authority for noble ideals. It is just as likely to let loose instincts of bestiality and evil desires.

> Mere anarchy is loosed upon the world
> The blood-dimmed tide is loosed.

It was Hitler who told us to think with our blood.

But to take ethics seriously is not to commit "the naturalistic fallacy", which is only an error attributed to a normal ethical judgment by someone who has got himself into a metaphysical muddle. If reality is really reduced to atoms in motion it cannot, of course, possess qualities of moral or any other value. It is absurd to look for them in what has been stripped of them. The only recourse is one or the other of the contemporary emotive theories of ethics which frankly state that the moral feeling is wholly a personal and a subjective one (as stated by Ayer and developed by Stevenson), or is a pronouncement of approval or disapproval, or a prescriptive statement (command) or some other linguistic description of moral speech.

But no one is suggesting as the answer that one should attach one's subjective judgments to non-ethical facts, or regard them as non-natural qualities. We must correct the initial mistake.

[19] G. E. Moore, *Ethics.*

"In analyzing or abstracting we are tearing asunder something which is homogeneous in its own nature; when we try to reconstruct the whole by putting together the elements thus surgically separated, we find that they have become refractory to being again united. When two different abstractions have been derived from one notion—for instance that of mechanisms and the qualities of the living being[20]—it is impossible to rebuild the integrated concept of the organism as a whole, by juxtaposing these two products of analysis."[21]

We are not suggesting any such procedure, which would indeed be to commit the naturalistic fallacy. We simply reject the initial dualism.

We are caught up in a cultural dualism which threatens to split man's personality as it has already fractured his institution. When we encounter such polarisation as mind and body, individual and society, fact and value—we must set ourselves the task of overcoming them as aspects of a seamless whole. Thought is not an attribute of pure spirit but a function of organisms with developed brains.

There can be no purely factual statements. All facts are diffused with value, and value diffused in facts. Neither nature nor life can be understood unless they are fused. We don't *have* to *fuse* them; they are in concrete experience always united. It is we who by our abstractions split them apart.

"all statements of fact, however free of evaluation they may seem, are possible *only* when some fundamental art of appraisal has already legislated for the manner of their entertainment, formulation and assertion. Instead, therefore, of separating judgments of fact from judgments of value as two mutually exclusive classes we must admit both factual and evaluating aspects in all judgments."[22]

There is only *one* world in which men and nature interact, and all perception of fact involves selection and evaluation. Prior

[20] Or of the purely molecular constitution of reality from that of its values.
[21] Agnes Arber, *The Mind and the Eye*.
[22] Marjorie Grene, *The Knower and the Known*.

points of view, the contribution of all past experience, remembered or implicit, are found in every judgment.[23]

The grounds for evaluation all arise *within* experience, and are socially constituted and developed, and as such are continously subject to rational criticism on the basis of experience, and sometimes to rejection or fundamental reconstruction. The supreme values are those which in human experience represent the realisation of our most sustained purposes and the satisfaction of our deepest and most permanent desires.

*Minds and Machines*

If the man is a machine, so is his brain; and for many people the supposed identity of brain and computer is a remarkable confirmation of this. While Monod does not venture into this question at all, mechanical thinking would certainly be the logical consequence of his mechanistic reduction of man.

There are indeed forms of thinking that are mechanical and can be done as well by machines as by brains. For these we use desk calculators, slide rules, cash registers and computers. But there are quite other kinds of thinking that machines cannot do at all, that transcend the mechanical tasks of machines. This is the thinking which depends on imagination. It is creative thinking.[24] In such thinking the mind creates various hypotheses, which are by no means logical inferences from the facts, and then tests them. Or we work out in our minds various alternative solutions or routes to a desired end coping with the envisaged difficulties, comparing them, estimating their consequences, balancing them and then deciding. We begin to think when we anticipate possible ways of reacting and consider tentative solutions.

Deliberation, self-criticism, planning, the imaginative invention of hypotheses, are mental processes that cannot be explained in purely physical terms, for they are neither *necessary* nor are they a matter of pure *chance*. Monod's dichotomy breaks down here.

The human brain is not a computer, nor does it work by simple trial and error—though it can, rather laboriously carry out the mechanical operations of the machine it is essentially an organ which, in Kuhn's terms, *shifts the paradigm* or pattern of thinking, from the

[23] See Polanyi on "implicit knowledge" in *The Structure of Consciousness* (in *The Anatomy of Knowledge*) and *The Tacit Dimension* (1966).
[24] Medawar, *Science and Literature*.

conventional one to an entirely new one. The essence of the computer is that it is restricted to its built-in paradigm, and cannot create a different one for itself.

Under the pressure of the recognition of anomalies and contradictions, insuperable obstacles and apparently insoluble problems, the mind re-creates the situation. It does not merely adapt to it. What we do is to invent a new theory, a new paradigm, and *submit it to critical examination.*[25] Man, unlike computers and animals, can reject a hundred hypotheses as inadequate. We proceed by making mistakes and knowing that we are mistaken.

Man is a curious kind of creature whose reactions are not determined from without by external pressures and his reactions to them, or from within by innate behaviour patterns and their conditioning, but by plans, purposes and intentions. These do not *act upon* the physical organism, it is the organism controlling itself. There is no stream of consciousness outside the physical organism. Man's bodily movements intervene in the course of events and release the organism's own energy, because *it* knew what the effect of the mechanical changes resulting were going to be before they occurred. Something has manipulated the series of physical events without adding energy or requiring it in such a way that one possible event followed rather than another, the expenditure of energy being the same in both cases. The human organism can drive his car from London to Cambridge or to Oxford according to the decision reached by his mind after weighing the pros and cons. It is his mental decision and takes no more energy to decide it one way as to decide it the other. This is freedom, and neither *chance* nor *necessity*.

[25] See Popper's essay "On Clouds and Clocks" in his *Objective Knowledge*.

CHAPTER EIGHT

# *How Much is Evolution affected by Chance and Necessity?*

C. H. WADDINGTON

I was not at the colloquium with Jacques Monod at the Royal Institution at which this book originated, but Dr. John Lewis invited me to contribute an article, and provoked me into giving an affirmative answer by telling me that Monod had accused me of being a Lysenkoist. This I take to have been a piece of semi-jocular abuse, of the kind one is used to and takes in good part from one's colleagues. I shall take it as licence to hit back equally hard at those parts of Monod's argument with which I disagree. I have already written a short review of the French edition of this book, and a still shorter one of the English translation, in the *Times Literary Supplement* employing the restrained language appropriate to the anonymity which that journal imposes.

First let me say that there are quite many parts of Monod's book for which I have great respect; in particular, those in which he deals with the genetic material, and with the importance of the global structures of macro-molecules in general. I also agree with him, rather than with most of the other contributors to this volume, in finding the writings of Teilhard du Chardin not at all to my taste, so that it is rather embarrassing to reply to him under these particular auspices.

My main concern is with Monod's ideas about evolution, and the interpretation I am told he places on my ideas on this subject. However, before coming to that there are a few preliminary points that I would like to make; in the first place about reductionism in general; second, about what Monod calls animism; and third, about his concluding remarks on the ethical basis of science.

The present debate between reductionism and "beyond reductionism" seems to me almost completely a re-run, for the second time round, of the controversy which in the 1920's and 1930's started by being between mechanists and vitalists, and finished by being between mechanists and "organicists". I agree now, as I did then, that the organicist view, which involves concepts such as integrative levels, organising relations, and the like, is much more powerful and useful than the strict mechanist view. (The merits of a dialectical materialism as opposed to a mechanical materialism, seems to me still unclear. It started off well in the hands of Engels, but that was a long time ago, and since then it has suffered the gross distortions afflicted on it by Lysenko, Prezent and others. It has, I think, never fully recovered from these.)

The argument I should like to advance, however, is that both the reductionists and the beyond-reductionists are seeing the situation upside down. They pose the problem in the form; does man, or any other biological organism, consist of physico-chemical atoms, or does he involve something more (such as organising relations or system properties arising at higher levels of integration, and the like)? This implies that the correct approach is to start with atoms or other physico-chemical notions, and to attempt to build up models of living things. I find myself returning more strongly to the opposite point of view, which I originally derived from Whitehead in the 1920's. This takes it that the basis of our knowledge is not in chemical entities and laws, but is in occasions of experience, which when systematically organised and observed can be rated as experiments.

Science is based not on mass, energy, atoms and the like, but on experiments, which involve an experimenter as well as the things he experiments with. The question we have to ask is not whether we have to add something to our well-known physical and chemical entities before we can explain biological phenomena, but rather whether, in deriving the slender knowledge we have acquired so far about atoms and molecules through physical and chemical experiments, we have been led to leave out something of their essential character, which we can learn about when we study their behaviour in biological contexts. When we do come across phenomena which do not follow from our previous knowledge of the physico-chemical entities—as, to take a relevant example, the allosteric behaviour of the tertiarty structure of proteins did not follow from the classical organic chemistry, or as quantum phenomena did not follow from classical physics—what we do is not to leave our ideas about atoms and molecules unchanged, and add something to them. Instead, we re-write our description of what we think an atom or molecule is, in such a way as to incorporate the new knowledge about them which we have derived from our new experiments. This is, if you like, to stand beyond-reductionism on its head.

Monod takes, as the type of erroneous thinking which he is most concerned to eradicate, a philosophy which he calls "animism". This he explains as an inclination—which he feels is unfortunately very deeply embedded in human nature—to envisage the forces and tendencies which man encounters in the natural world as being the characteristics of persons. In its most explicit form, animism "explains" a situation by telling a story of how certain personal beings brought about the situation by their willed actions—as Adam and Eve initiated the growth of human understanding by plucking the fruit of the Tree of Knowledge. Monod argues that it is of the first importance for any genuine (i.e. operationally effective and intellectually satisfying) understandng of the natural world to abolish any reference to such mythological personalised concepts, and to use language and ideas in which the name of a concept refers only and unequivocally to a precisely definable referendum. It is a fine challenging thesis, very much akin to that put forward by, for instance, the Viennese positivists such as Karnap, who wanted to reduce the whole of knowledge to the manipulation of atomic statements. Personally, I do not believe that it is a practical proposition. I do not think that language is that kind of instrument; and I do not think that the knowledge about the world which we derive from the occasions when we perceive it has that kind of character.

But this is too big a subject to be argued in detail here. I just want to make the perhaps rather flippant comment that the English speaker tends to lift a slightly amused eyebrow when confronted with someone who is attempting to abolish animism, and is using a language in which Chance and Necessity have genders. Le Hazard et La Nécessité? Well, Chance I suppose has usually been considered masculine; its ruling power would be somebody like Hermes, or in India Ganesh, an elephant-headed but definitely male character; and in German it is *der* Zufall. And, of course, there is no doubt at all about Necessity. The Greek Fates—Clotho, Atropos and Lachesis, were certainly women, and so were the Germanic Norns. I personally should admit that the embroideries on the basic concepts implied by these attributions of sexuality are suggestive, and not without value if not taken too seriously; but the point I am making is that a language in which they are deeply embedded in the basic grammar is a rather unconvincing vehicle to use to put forward arguments for wholly abolishing them. If Jacques Monod is to stop being animist he will have to cease speaking and writing French!

In Monod's last chapter he claims that the scientific enterprise—the attempt to understand the natural world in the way in which science attempts this task—rests on a fundamental act of belief that this is something worth doing. Science, he argues, attempts to keep ethical considerations out of its day-to-day involvement with detailed situations, but does so only on the basis of a fundamentally ethical prejudgement about the foundations on which it has to stand. I agree, up to a point, but I should like to claim that I have gone further. So far as I can see, I was making very much the same point in the last chapter, called "Believing in Science" in one of my earlier books, *The Scientific Attitude*, written in 1941. But in later books, such as *The Ethical Animal, The Nature of Life* and *Biology Purpose and Ethics* I have tried to show that the ethical judgment on which science is based is not just an arbitrary matter, which you can choose one way or another as fancy takes you.

In one of his more assertive flights of rhetoric, Monod claims that he is a follower of Descartes, and asserts boldly that "man is a machine". But a machine is defined as a physical system put together by a designer or manufacturer in order to carry out certain predetermined processes. If man is literally a machine he must have a designer. Descartes was, at least officially, a Deist, and could accept this conclusion with no qualms. But Monod? I suspect that what he means is that man is a machine-like system which has been assembled, not according to any thought-out design, but by the processes of evolution through natural selection. If this is what he means, I should agree with him; but I think that Monod's ideas about how evolution brings about such a result are completely out of date. They are the orthodoxy of the 1920's and 1930's. He is trying to freeze our blood by rattling the same old bones that Fisher and Haldane used to deck themselves out as terrifying witch-doctors who could conjure the souls out of the bodies of the innocently religious. These ideas are just not good enough, though there may still be some novelty about them in France, a country which allowed a somewhat chauvinistic devotion to Lamark and Bergson to cloud its perception of the importance of Darwin, and which has remained rather remarkably far behind the forefront of thought about evolutionary matters for at least the last half century.

Monod's insistence on the importance of Chance and Necessity as guiding forces in evolution, and his dismissal of my work as "Lysenkoist", should be seen in the context of the general development of evolutionary thought since the rediscovery of Mendel. People sometimes write as though this had followed a single consistent course, leading up to a climatic theory called synthetic neo-Darwinism, enshrined in such works as Julian Huxley's *Evolution: the Modern Synthesis*. Actually the passage has been much less smooth. There have been several quite radical changes of viewpoint, some perhaps drastic and far-reaching enough to be considered changes of "paradigm", of the kind discussed by Kuhn.

Certainly the change in evolutionary thinking introduced by the rediscovery of Mendel and the basic laws of genetics, in the very first years of this century, amounted to a shift of paradigm. At the time it occurred, the dominant ideas about heredity were those promulgated by authors such as Galton and Pearson. These were essentially phrased in statistical terms, and dealt with the similarities between classes of related individuals—offspring and parents or grandparents, first cousins and so on. The rediscovered Mendelism not only introduced the notion of separate discrete hereditary factors or genes, but also emphasised the importance of studying hereditary phenomena in crosses between individual organisms, and of observing the characteristics of individual offspring. One of the main bones of contention in the fierce battles that raged between the early Mendelians and the followers of Pearson is just the fact that the new paradigm insisted on the importance of studying individuals, and rejected, as unimportant or irrelevant, any consideration of statistical aggregates. This rejection was so drastic that Udny Yule's mathematical demonstration, that the statistical rules advocated by Pearson could actually be produced from the Mendelian laws if one supposed that complex characters, such as height, may be affected by many Mendelian genes, passed almost unnoticed and was allowed to become almost forgotten.

The first Mendelian paradigm also laid stress on the importance of the processes of mutation by which individual genes occasionally change. It was unfortunate that one of the rediscoverers of Mendelism, de Vries had chosen as his experimental subject the evening primrose,

*Oenothera*. Many species of this genus have a habit of suddenly throwing up new and unexpected hereditary variants. These were interpreted as examples of mutation, and this tended to emphasise the important effects that mutations might produce in the appearance of new varieties, and also the random character of the process itself. It was not until many years later that it was shown, largely by C. D. Darlington, that *Oenothera* has a most unusual genetic system, involving an elaborate series of exchanges of parts between different chromosomes, and that de Vries' mutations were a very special phenomenon, depending essentially on the recombination within chromosomes, rather than being typical of gene mutations in general. However, it was in this very earliest version of the Mendelian paradigm that the "chance variations", which Darwin had invoked as the raw materials of evolution, became translated into terms of random mutations of genes.

Perhaps it is as well to say a word here about the meaning of "random" in this context. Gene mutation is certainly not random in any complete sense. A few decades ago it was considered that the gene is a highly complex molecule, held in a given stable configuration only by quantum chemical forces and liable to shift from one such position of temporary stability to another, as unpredictably and indeed non-deterministically as electrons may behave in an atom. But we now know that the gene consists of a string of nucleotides, of which there are only four kinds. Only certain types of change are possible. Mutation can consist of moving one or more bases from the string, or insertion of one or more additional ones, or the substitution of one nucleotide in place of another at a given location. These are quite definite chemical processes, the mechanics of which can be studied and eventually understood in strictly causal terms. But although we know a great deal about the kind of changes that may occur, and although the study of the causal mechanisms involved is a very active research field, this does not completely remove the grounds for referring to mutation as "random in the context of evolution". What is meant by that expression is that the alterations produced in a gene, and the effects which this alteration will have on the phenotype of the individual which develops under its influence, are not causally connected with the natural selective forces which will determine its success or failure in producing offspring in the next generation. What we have learnt about the causal mechanisms of mutation in fact reinforces the conclusion that the sorts of environmental influences which affect natural selective pressures can have nothing to do with the induction of mutations appropriate to meet those pressures.

Returning to our main theme, the first Mendelian paradigm, of individual genes in the individual organisms, which was championed by writers like Bateson and Morgan for a quarter of a century, was then superseded by a view centred on populations rather than on individuals, but still dealing mainly with single identifiable genes. The main advocates for this new paradigm were Fisher, Haldane and to some extent Sewall Wright (athough he perhaps belongs more to the third paradigm, discussed below). Just how drastic was the change of emphasis between the first and second of these Mendelian or neo-Darwinist paradigms will be apparent when we discuss later the case of the notorious experiments of Kammerer. But now let us press on to the third paradigm, which followed only about ten years after the second. This shift of emphasis which is most appropriately associated with the name of Dobzhansky, emphasised that evolution has to be thought of in terms not only of populations of organisms, but of populations of genes.

Previously it had been held, with gradually diminishing conviction, that in a population of animals or plants in nature, nearly all individuals had essentially the same hereditary constitution, referred to as "wild-type". It was realised that a wild-type appearance might conceal one or two recessive genes, but mutant genes were thought of as essentially rarities, which could be distinguished sharply from a background of uniformity. Sewall Wright in theory, and Dobzhansky in particular in experimental studies of wild populations, demonstrated that the situation is quite different. Any individual in a population differs from every other in many genes. There is no uniform wild type. We have to think of the population as containing a pool of genes, from which each individual draws its particular complement, and returns them again to the pool when mating with another individual and producing offspring.

Thus both the main items of the first post-Mendelian paradigm—individual organisms, and individual genes—had been drastically changed by the time neo-Darwinism completed its development. In the first step the emphasis on individual organisms was replaced by emphasis on populations and a return of statistical methods of thought; and then the emphasis on individual genes became changed to a consideration of gene pools, in which the individual components lose much of their prime importance. These are the three successive variants of the Neo-Darwinist paradigm.

There is another basically different paradigm, which we need to take into consideration before discussing Monod's views about Chance and Necessity and my alleged Lysenkoism. This is the view which I began to put forward in the very early 1940's, and which has since been developed, with a good deal of experimental as well as theoretical work, mainly by myself and my colleagues and students such as J. M. Rendel, Alex Fraser, Gillian Bateman, Evelyn Robertson and others. I have sometimes referred to it as post-neo-Darwinism; but it might also be called the Epigenetic paradigm, because its central point is that natural selection does not operate directly on genotypes, but instead on phenotypes which are produced by epigenetic processes in which the environment as well as the genotype plays a part.

In all the neo-Darwinist paradigms, from Bateson and Morgan, through Fisher and Haldane to Sewall Wright and Dobzhansky, discussion was all in terms of natural selection and genes, or genotypes, or gene pools. When one mentions phenotypes—if the antelope has to escape from the lion by running away, the crucial point is not what genes it contains, but how fast can it run? Neo-Darwinists tend to lift their noses from their algebra or computers and say "Of course, of course, we have to introduce some sort of a fudge factor; heritability is not always 100%; we are dealing with fuzzy variables; we have to map the situation into a tolerance space. But don't get excited, there is nothing to it, it just makes things go on slightly slower, that's all."

The epigenetic paradigm says that this won't do at all. These arguments are based on the supposition that the effect of an unusual environment on phenotypes is "random", in the same sense as we argued above that its effect on gene mutation is random, it implicitly postulates that when you transfer your attention from genotypes to phenotypes, all that happens is that the natural selective value of the genotype becomes blurred isotropically over a greater or smaller circle centred on the phenotypic value. But this is exactly what does *not* occur. As a matter of empirical observation, we know that when unusual environmental circumstances succeed in modifying the phenotype of an organism, the resulting modification is, far more frequently than would be expected on a random basis, of such a kind as to improve natural selective fitness. Biological organisms have a strong tendency to *adapt* epigenetically and phenotypically to the environments they meet. Even bacteria, as Monod knows much more thoroughly than I do, can often react epigenetically to the presence of an unusual substrate in their environment by producing a phenotype which is better able to survive and multiply in that particular medium.

This argument results in a very drastic change in the paradigm which has insisted that the factors which produce evolutionarily important changes are quite unrelated to those which determine whether those changes will persist and contribute effectively to the direction in which evolution proceeds. The environmental factors which exert natural selective pressure do not, as we saw above, have any important tendency to produce appropriate changes in the genotype, but they do very often tend to produce appropriate alterations of the phenotype, and it is on the phenotype, not on the genotype, that natural selection operates.

This is only one of the cherished neo-Darwinist myths which the epigenetic paradigm calls in question. It goes on to ask: what determines the nature of the natural selective pressures to which any given range of phenotypes will be subjected? There will be many determining factors—the climate, the soil, predator species, parasitical species, in fact the whole of some ecosystem or other; but it is surely very clear that the phenotypes which are going to be selected are also amongst the determinants. Just which ecosystem are they going to try to operate in? There is always the possibility that at least some members of a population may decide to opt out and try something else. Some mammals, at some point in evolutionary history, must have said "to hell with all this dry land stuff, let's take to the sea", and become whales, dolphins and so on; and some birds forgot all about flying, and subjected themselves to particular natural selective pressures which caused them to evolve into ostriches.

In the neo-Darwinist paradigms, we have genotypes or gene pools subject to mutational alterations "at random", and to natural selection by external forces unrelated to the character of the things they have to select. In the epigenetic paradigm we have to contemplate a subtle system of feedbacks, in which the environmental factors which exert natural selection operate on phenotypes which they themselves have influenced in relevant ways (usually to improve their effectiveness), and in which the phenotypes in their turn have an influence on the nature of the natural selective pressures to which they will be subject.

Now we are about ready to tackle Jacques Monod's "Chance". In the genotype-centred neo-Darwinist paradigms it was a key point in the first Bateson-Morgan phase, and retained much of its importance in the second Haldane-Fisher phase. But by the time we had got to Dobzhansky and gene pools, its relevance was becoming more restricted. If you are concerned with some characteristic very closely connected with a primary gene—for instance, whether there is an arginine rather than a theonine at position X in some specific protein—then this does basically depend on whether the "random" processes of gene mutation have produced in the population a species of DNA with the right set of nucleotides to code for the particular amino acid you want at that point. In so far as these considerations hold, Chance is still important; but surely they do not hold very much in the evolution of higher organisms. If the antelope needs to run faster, if the whale needs to swim better, success must very rarely be dependent on a precise amino-acid substitution in one particular protein.

The gene pool of a population can offer an enormous number of slightly varying building blocks, and out of these some assemblages can be made which will meet the natural selective criteria with reasonable efficiency. The "random" nature of the processes which produced the elementary building blocks comes to be unimportant when the building blocks are employed in statistically large aggregates. I have in this connection used the analogy of architecture in reinforced concrete. It is perfectly true that the individual units, the stones, gravel, sand, incorporated into the concrete, have been produced by random processes, but the character of the architecture is dependent in only a very minor degree on the nature of the aggregate which the architect specifies for his mix. Similarly the gene variants fed into the gene pool of a population may with due caution, be said to have been produced by "random" processes, but this fact becomes almost irrelevant when we are concerned with the nature of evolutionary changes between, say, *Eohippus* and the modern horse, or the primitive primates and man.

Thus as evolutionary theory moved into the orbit of Dobzhansky, Chance gradually lost the domination position it had had for Bateson. Within the epigenetic paradigm it plays an even more subordinate role. The central focus of interest shifts to the type of natural selection which acts on phenotypes in a cybernetic situation in which environment affects phenotypes and phenotypes chose environments—as in the selection for speed of running of animals which choose to escape their predators by flight. The basic biochemical variants which genuinely do depend on chance mutations, such as the position of particular amino acid residues at specific points in a primary protein chain, appear of as very little consequence indeed. In the higher stages of the evolutionary progression—and by higher I mean from bacteria inclusive upwards—Le Hazard has to be content with a very back seat role.

Let us turn now to Necessity. Monod makes it clear that when he says that evolution follows a *necessary* course, this does not imply that it follows a *predictable* course. He does, however, assume that the necessity which exerts the pressure of natural selection on a population arises always outside of and external to it. This is also the implication of all the neo-Darwinist paradigms—at least they do not explicitly discuss ways in which the character of necessity might depend on the character of the organisms subjected to it. These considerations are raised as an important issue by the epigenetic paradigm. It argues that we are confronted here by a circular or cybernetic set of relationships, in which the phenotypes resulting from previous natural selection have a strong influence on the character of the natural selection to which they themselves will be subject. "Necessity" is a very inadequate term in this context.

Finally, what about "the inheritance acquired characters", and the alleged Lamarckian or Lysenkoist tendencies of the epigenetic paradigm? The first point to note is that the whole of this topic essentially demands an epigenetic approach. An "acquired character" must be in the first place a phenotypic character, a result of epigenesis.

The conventional response to the suggestion of the inheritance of acquired characters was formulated in the days of the first neo-Darwinist paradigm, when the emphasis was on genotypes rather than on phenotypes, and on the genotypes of single individuals at that. The crucial question was interpreted to be; if an individual organism, subjected to an unusual environment during its development, develops a phenotype different from that which would be expected in normal circumstances, will there be an increased probability that a similar phenotype will be exhibited by that individual's offspring? The answer has been no, on two grounds. First, that nobody has been able to produce any experimental evidence in favour of the hypothesis. Second, our understanding of the mechanisms of genetics suggest no way in which such a process might be supposed to occur; it suffices, for instance to exclude Darwin's hypothesis of "pangenes". This still remains the situation, and I would not want to quarrel with it—or not much.[1]

[1] Some geneticists, such as Bateson, and many orthodox neo-Darwinists, get so hot under the collar at the mention of the inheritance of acquired characters that they stimulate those who dislike dogmas to try to think of ways to escape this one. At one time, just before the discovery that the gene consists of DNA and the elucidation of the structure of that molecule, I offered a speculation about a possible mechanism for the inheritance of a character acquired by an individual. It was based on the supposition that the gene consists of protein, or something like that. It has clearly now become quite untenable, and the suggestion should be consigned to oblivion.

However, I still dislike dogmas, so I will offer another outrageous speculation. We have recently learned that the genotypes of higher organisms contain many nearly identical replicates of certain genetic elements. This seems quite certain for stretches of DNA which code for certain of the important RNAs involved in the manufacture of proteins, such as the ribosomal RNAs, tRNAs, etc. It has been thought there may also be replicates of structural genes coding for proteins, but this is not yet so definitely established. In so far as such replicate genes occur, a genotype must be considered not just as a collection of individual genes, but as a collection of populations of genes. Moreover, the cell contains another population of genetic elements, namely those in the mitochondria, of which most cells contain several, and the egg cells in particular usually very large numbers. As we are dealing with populations, there could be selection among the individuals of the population.

We know almost nothing about the rates of multiplication of slightly different replicate genes, or of slightly different forms of mitochondrial genes. However, since these genes or their products are very closely involved with many of the most important metabolic processes of the cells, it is by no means *a priori* impossible to suppose that the rates of multiplication of slightly differing genes would be influenced by the particular metabolic circumstances reigning in the cell in question. It seems to be not inconceivable that the imposition of certain metabolic conditions on an organism might change the proportion of mutant forms of gene within the population to be passed on to the next generation. In fact, I should even think it quite probable that we could in this way change the proportions of mitochondria carrying different mutant mitochondrial genes. If such processes can occur—and, of course, at present they are purely speculative and there is no definite evidence for them, but then nobody has yet searched for any—the effect would appear as a direct inheritance of a character acquired by an individual.

The response of most neo-Darwinists to this argument—and I daresay it would be Monod's response too—is to say "this is unfair, of course, you can get selection within populations, but we are not talking about that sort of inheritance of acquired characters". The point is that this is the kind of phenomenon in which evolution is interested. Evolution is about populations. The refusal to countenance the "inheritance of acquired characters" has become a dogma because it has been seen primarily not in the context of evolution, but in that of the nature of genetic determinants, the context of Weisman and molecular biology.

There is one further conceivable stage in the mechanism of the evolution of adapted phenotypes. What will happen if the environment changes again, and the circumstances which elicited the adapted phenotypes in the first place no longer persists? The answer to this comes from our general knowledge of the processes of epigenesis. They tend to be buffered or canalised, that is to say resistant to change. If an altered environment is drastic enough to produce an altered phenotype in at least some members of a population, and if this phenotype is adaptive and is selected over a number of generations, the development of the adaptive phenotype may itself become buffered and resistant to later alteration when the original precipitating

But, as even later neo-Darwinist paradigms recognised, evolution is not mainly concerned with individuals, but with populations. In so far as the inheritance of acquired characters has any evolutionary importance, the problem should be phrased in terms of populations. And put in those terms, it looks exceedingly different. The question becomes; if unusual circumstances cause the appearance of unusual phenotypes, in a population subjected to them, will this increase the frequency with which similar phenotypes will appear in the population of the next generation? The answer must surely and obviously be "Yes, usually". This follows from three things which are rather firmly known about populations. One, organisms usually react to abnormal environments in ways which are adaptive, that is to say which increase their probability of leaving offspring. Two, there will be natural selection for those individuals which do adapt most successfully. Three, there will be some genetic component contributing to the appearance of the adapted phenotypes. "The inheritance of acquired characters" is nowadays generally recognised as being a loose and basically inadmissible phrase. Perhaps, with the same degree of looseness, I may be allowed to say: "Characters acquired by individuals are

---

circumstances are removed. I have used the phrase "genetic assimilation" to refer to this situation, and I and some of my students, such as Bateman, have shown that it does in fact occur in certain experimental situations, either when the selection is exerted by a human abnormal environment, such as that produced by the presence of excess salt in the medium on which Drosophila larvae are living.

Thus a combination of the epigenetic paradigm with a general population outlook leads one to expect the occurrence of a process which, on the population level, gives a result similar to that which the inheritance of acquired characters in the classical sense was supposed to give on the individual level; and the expected process does in practice occur. It is, however, perfectly orthodox genetics combined with a bit of orthodox embryology. I do not see that any purpose is served by calling it Lamarckist. Lamarck himself, of course, was working with a theory of biology very far removed from Mendelian theories of evolution, while the doctrines attributed to him more recently had been phrased in terms of the first neo-Darwinist paradigm of individuals. Even more irrelevant is the reference to Lysenko. His outlook, as far as we in the West can discover it, was certainly in terms of some individual paradigm. Some Russian authors belonging to the non-Lysenko school of genetics, particularly Schmalhausen, began developing a general epigenetic paradigm about evolution about the same time that I did, but probably just because of the existence of Lysenko they didn't work out the theory of genetic assimilation thoroughly either in theory or in practice.

The implications of the epigenetic paradigm for our general notions about evolution can perhaps be indicated by suggesting an alternative to Monod's slogan. Out of the rhetoric of the neo-Darwinist myth that evolution is brought about by the natural selection of random gene mutations, he produces the phrase "Chance and Necessity". From a cooler look at phenotypes, epigenesis, populations and behaviour, which sees evolution as the result of natural selection of phenotypes which tend to be adapted to what they allow to select them, one would arrive rather at something like "Learning and Innovation".

not inherited by their individual offspring but characters acquired by populations are inherited by their offspring populations if they are adaptive."

The few cases which have been claimed in the past to demonstrate the inheritance of acquired characters can almost certainly be interpreted in this way, namely as the result of selection. For instance, in Kammerer's famous midwife-toad work, he started his experiments with several hundred and finished with only three or four, so the selection pressures involved must have been enormous. But such was the dominance of the first neo-Darwinist emphasis on individuals that no one could look at the matter in population terms.

CHAPTER NINE

# *Interpreting Molecular Biology*[1]

ROBIN E. MONRO

In *Chance and Necessity* Jacques Monod deploys his specialised knowledge of molecular biology[2] to provide what is prima facie a convincing case for certain propositions of a social and philosophical nature. Most of Monod's critics have accepted his technical arguments on authority and contented themselves with pointing out flaws in his general arguments. In this article I try to show that Monod's technical arguments also contain significant flaws, which can be exposed by analysis from the standpoint of molecular biology itself. These flaws lead to distortions in Monod's conception of organisms.

Monod starts out by proposing that living organisms are distinguishable from the rest of the universe by three general characteristics: teleonomy, autonomous morphogenesis and reproductive invariance. Teleonomy denotes the characteristic "*of being objects endowed with a purpose or project,* which at the same time they exhibit in their structure and carry out through their performances". (The term *teleonomic* was introduced by Pittendrigh[3] as a descriptive term for all end-directed systems "not committed to Aristotelian teleology", i.e., to the operation of final causes.) Autonomous morphogenesis denotes the formation of a highly structured object (organism) not from the action of outside forces but through morphogenetic interactions within the object itself. Reproductive invariance denotes the capacity of organisms to reproduce and transmit the information corresponding to their own structure. Monod goes on to suggest that,

[1] This is a modified and extended version of an article which appeared in the *Cambridge Review, 94* (October, 1972), p. 20.
[2] Throughout this article, the term *molecular biology* is used in a broad sense, intended to include other related disciplines, such as biochemistry, biophysics and cell biology.
[3] C. S. Pittendrigh, in *Behaviour and Evolution,* A. Roe and G. G. Simpson, Eds. (Yale Univ. Press: New Haven, 1958), p. 394.

> ... these three concepts do not all have the same standing. Whereas invariance and teleonomy are indeed characteristic "properties" of living beings, spontaneous structuration ought rather to be considered a mechanism ... this mechanism intervenes both in the elaboration of teleonomic structures and in the reproduction of invariant information. That it finally accounts for the latter two properties does not, however, imply that they should be regarded as one ... it is methodologically indispensable—to maintain a distinction between them ... this distinction is assumed, explicitly or otherwise, in all theories, all ideological constructions (religious, scientific, or philosophical) pertaining to the biosphere and to its relationship to the rest of the universe.
>
> (pp. 26–27)[4]

Monod submits that the central problem of biology lies in the apparent contradiction between the teleonomic character of living organisms and the basic postulate of modern science, which he defines as the objectivity of nature and the "systematic denial that 'true' knowledge can be reached by interpreting phenomena in terms of final causes ...". He considers the dilemma to be resolvable if it can be shown that (*a*) the teleonomic properties of organisms are a consequence of underlying structures, and are explicable in terms of chemical and physical mechanisms, and (*b*) such structures arise through natural selection: i.e., "the initial appearance, evolution, and steady refinement of ever more intensely teleonomic structures are due to perturbations occurring in a structure *which already possesses the property of* [reproductive] *invariance*—hence is capable of preserving the effects of chance and thereby submitting them to the play of natural selection." According to the author, all other hypotheses as to the nature of life (including those of all religions, most cultures and many philosophies) are vitalist or animist and assume the reverse of this.

Monod's categories of autonomous morphogenesis and reproductive invariance themselves need further examination. Likewise, his imparting of primacy to invariance over teleonomy raises certain questions. However, for the moment I shall concentrate on the way he develops his thesis. He argues that the concept of natural selec-

[4] All page numbers refer to the English edition of Jacques Monod's *Chance and Necessity* (Collins: London, 1972).

tion was more or less correctly formulated by Darwin but that its final acceptance had to await elucidation of the mechanisms underlying the reproduction and functioning of organisms. Let us examine this thesis a little more closely. In the first place it is certainly true that molecular biology has strengthened certain aspects of Darwinism, and has increased the coherence of biology. Thus, the discovery of remarkable similarities among biological molecules and systems of molecules throughout nature provides very convincing corroboration of the (already convincing) evidence from palaeontology that living organisms have evolved from a common ancestor—and have extended the scope of this generalisation to micro-organisms and viruses. Moreover, by providing certain bridges between biology and the physical sciences, molecular biology has increased the coherence of science as a whole. Thus, the processes whereby energy is derived and utilised for biosynthesis, movement and other functions can now be thought of in physico-chemical terms, and have become as much the domain of the physical scientist as of the biologist. The same can be said concerning certain aspects of reproduction, especially those at the molecular level.

In spite of such considerable advances, it must not be forgotten that our knowledge of organisms is still extremely fragmentary. There is plenty of scope left for revolutions to occur in biology (as is discussed below). Nevertheless, I am inclined to think that molecular biology does support Darwinism in the global sense of strengthening mechanistic biology as a whole—but not in a direct way. The concepts of neo-Darwinism were formulated largely before the rise of molecular biology and depend primarily upon evidence from population genetics. By elucidating certain underlying mechanisms and providing a model for gene action molecular biology only refines a system of explanation which was already widely accepted in biology. Monod, it appears, would only partially go along with this view: he wants to elevate the contribution of molecular biology to that of *proof* rather than corroboration and refinement. I believe that Monod is mistaken in trying to do this, and that there are certain recurrent types of fallacy in his arguments. In order to expose these it will be necessary to examine his interpretation of molecular biology in some detail.

*Chemical arguments*

In connection with his three categories, Monod maintains that,

The distinction between teleonomy and invariance is more

> than a mere logical abstraction. *It is warranted on the grounds of chemistry.* Of the two basic classes of biological macromolecules, one, that of proteins, is responsible for almost all teleonomic structures and performances; while genetic invariance is linked exclusively to the other class, that of nucleic acids.
>
> p. 27
> (italics are mine)

Monod uses chemical arguments at more than one point to "prove" general principles. Such arguments reflect a predilection to give undue primacy to the molecular level (an example of Whitehead's "fallacy of misplaced concreteness").

As regards invariance and DNA, it is certainly true that DNA is a remarkably stable and replicably faithful store of high density information. Moreover, the existence of such a store may be an essential prerequisite for the occurrence of organisms. However, it is a big jump from there to the assertion (p. 108) that the characteristics of DNA explain the occurrence of such phenomena as species-stability. Monod, himself, points out as an afterthought (footnote, p. 108), that the explanation of this phenomenon is to be sought not only in the stability of DNA, but also in "the extreme coherence of the teleonomic system" (p. 117) and the action of natural selection thereon. In fact, contemporary geneticists believe that species stability is something of a myth; that the DNA of a species continually changes in small ways from one generation to another, while the gross structure of the organisms may remain relatively constant. This is possible because *similar phenotypes can arise from different genotypes*. Invariance in the gross morphology of a species is not to be attributed only to the invariance of its DNA but, also, to the adaptedness of a particular phenotype to prevailing environmental conditions. In one set of conditions a species will remain stable, in another it will differentiate. Ecological relationships must be afforded a place of equal and complementary significance to that of molecular mechanisms in the explanation of constancy and change in evolution.

The identification of teleonomy with proteins is equally misleading. Monod passes over the fact that only certain segments of DNA, i.e., *structural genes*, specify proteins. Other segments express their information without doing this (for example the *operator*: a type of *regulator gene*, that helps to control the production of proteins by structural genes). And even in the case of structural genes, the information is not expressed solely through the proteins they specify but also partly through properties of the DNA itself (and of the messenger RNA). A recent commentary in *Nature*[5] begins with the remark, "Gone are the days when DNA was seen as nothing more than a repository of information . . ." and proceeds to suggest that, ". . . allosterism is now beginning to engulf DNA". (The role of secondary structure of messenger RNA in controlling its rate of translation has already been accepted for some time.) Teleonomic expression of genetic information must thus be attributed to properties of DNA (and RNA) as well as to those of proteins. All such properties must be taken into account in relating the molecular level to that of whole organisms. Moreover, relations between the properties of molecules and the character states of whole organisms are of a highly indirect nature (it is this that makes possible the concurrence of similar phenotypes with different genotypes). For this and other reasons it is not possible to specify, precisely, what all the teleonomic expressions of a given gene are.

*Autonomous morphogenesis*

I have tried to show that Monod's chemical argument for the distinction between teleonomy and invariance does not bear close scrutiny. In the next section I shall examine another chemical argument used by Monod; but first let us look more closely at his conception of *autonomous morphogenesis* (from which he considers teleonomy and invariance to derive). Monod views morphogenesis as a fixed mechanism. Here, I believe, is another source of confusion. Morphogenesis is *not* autonomous. While we do believe that the sequential information in the DNA of a given organism is more or less fixed (not entirely, as we shall see), and that the structures of the protein molecules specified thereby are also fixed, the relative extents to which the different genes are *expressed* (as, e.g. in protein synthesis) is only partly fixed. There is a complex, hierarchical relationship between the properties of nucleic acids and proteins, on the one hand, and the character states of whole organisms, on the other hand; and the structure of this relationship is only partly dictated by the information in DNA. It is also influenced by the environment, through the controlling action of external influences on the expression of individual genes and sets of genes. The gross morphology of an organism is, no doubt, dictated by its genome

[5] *Nature*, *241*, 502 (1973).

(genetic inheritance) but environmental influences during epigenesis play a very significant part in modulating the structure, especially in higher organisms and in the later stages of epigenesis (in which learning processes become important). The genetic information of an organism should not be looked upon as a blueprint for the organism but, rather, as a set of algorithms or instructions for assembling and maintaining the organism in conjunction with environmental impacts. It is highly misleading to think of an organism as a fixed machine whose structure is entirely predetermined by its genome. The importance of this point will become more apparent as we come to consider evolution and behaviour.

*Central Dogma*

The climax to Monod's theme, identifying invariance with DNA and teleonomy with proteins, comes in his interpretation of a principle of molecular biology, sometimes referred to as Crick's *central dogma*.[6] This principle states (in simplified form) that information can flow from DNA to DNA (replication) or from DNA to protein (protein synthesis but not from protein to DNA (Figs. 1*a–c*). It is here, especially, that Monod supposes molecular biology to provide direct proof of the primacy of invariance over teleonomy. He considers the irreversibility

[6] F. H. C. Crick, *Nature, 227*, 561 (1970).

---

Fig. 1. Crick's *central dogma*. Arrows indicate the directional flow of detailed, sequential information among the three families of informational polymers, DNA, RNA and protein. Circular arrows indicate self-replication.

(*a*) All the possible simple transfers.

(*b*) A tentative classification for the present day, embodying the central dogma.

(*c*) The simplified scheme dealt with in the text. The blocked arrows indicate that proteins can neither self-replicate nor pass their information to DNA. Discussion of RNA and its role as an information *messenger* between DNA and protein is avoided in the main argument for purposes of simplicity. The argument would follow much the same lines if RNA were included in it.

(*d*) Known information-transfers between DNA and RNA. Most RNA molecules function as *messengers*, but a few, notably ribosomal RNA and transfer RNA, do not act as messengers but perform functional and structural roles analogous to those of proteins. There is no indication that information transfer from these molecules to DNA does, in fact, take place, but it could do in principle—and it may have done during the early stages of evolution.

(Figs. 1*a* and 1*b* are redrawn from *Nature, 227*, 561 (1970) by kind permission of Dr. F. H. C. Crick and the editor of *Nature*.)

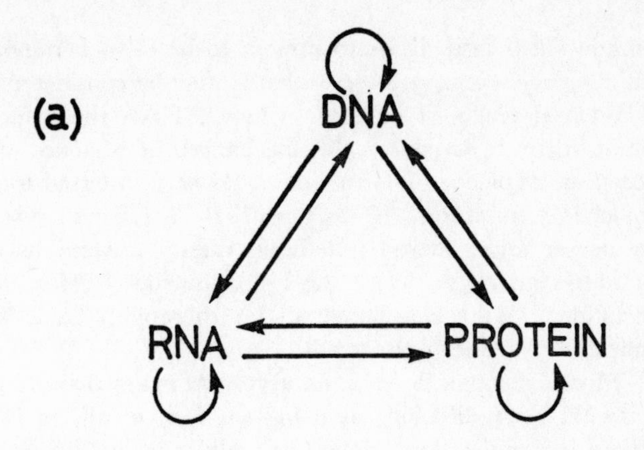


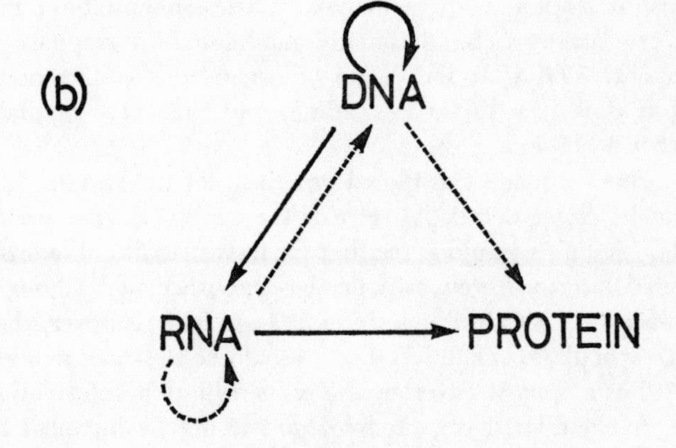


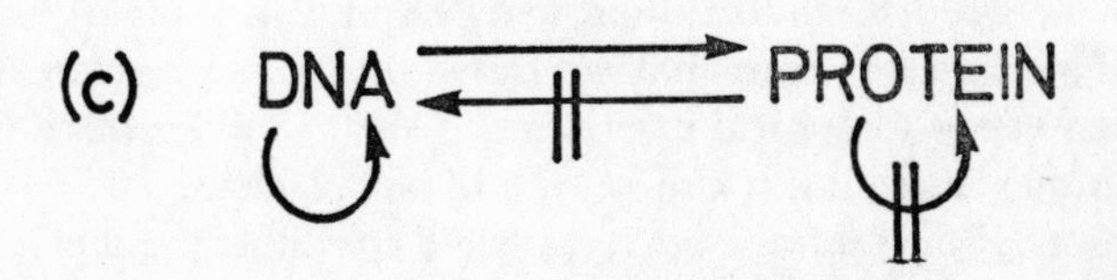


(d) DNA ⇄ RNA

of information-flow from DNA to protein to be of such importance, "especially for evolutionary theory—that it may be considered one of the fundamental tenets of modern biology". From the principle it follows that "there is no conceivable mechanism in existence whereby any instruction or piece of information could be transferred to DNA" except by chance mutations. "Consequently the entire system is totally intensely conservative, locked into itself, utterly impervious to any 'hints' from the outside world . . . this system obviously defies 'dialectical' description. It is not Hegelian at all, but thoroughly Cartesian: the cell is indeed a machine" (pp. 107–8).

Monod does not develop this argument in any detail. I believe that he would have difficulty in doing so. First of all, as we have already seen, it is misleading to look upon cells as being "impervious to any 'hints' from the outside world". If the organism is to be considered a machine, it is not a fixed machine in a Cartesian sense but a machine whose very structure is continually modulated in response to the environment. The Cartesian view of organisms, as interpreted by Monod, is thus seen to be misleading, and the value of dialectical approaches becomes apparent.

Having made this global criticism, let us examine Monod's argument in closer detail. As regards the central dogma itself, most molecular biologists would agree that the irreversibility of information-flow from DNA to protein is a firmly established fact (though even Crick, himself, is not absolutely committed to it).[6] However, there has been little speculation as to whether it should be regarded as a general, theoretical principle. In my view the irreversibility of information-flow is more closely related to principles underlying biochemical mechanisms, systems theory and simple mathematics (there is a degenerate relation between the information in DNA and in protein),[7] than to issues of mechanism versus vitalism, Darwinism versus Lamarckism, or Cartesian versus dialectical description. I shall consider three ways in which Monod's argument can be seen to be fallacious.

1. If the central dogma really did constitute proof of Monod's thesis, then the corollary should also hold: i.e., the occurrence of *reversibility* of information-flow between DNA and proteins would disprove Monod's thesis and open the way to purposive effects in evoluton. Monod would then be in serious trouble, for despite his footnote (pp. 107–8) to the contrary, the discovery of the *reverse tran-*

[7] R. E. Monro, to be published.

*scriptase* does affect his argument. This enzyme permits the transfer of information from RNA to DNA, and since the end-products of certain genes are RNA molecules (with structural and functional roles analogous to those of proteins), information could be transferred back from certain gene products (or modifications of them) to the genes that specify them (Fig. 1*d*). The situation is thus comparable to what it would be if information could flow back from a protein to the gene specifying it. In point of fact, I do not believe that this disproves Monod's overall thesis but, rather, that it illustrates the irrelevance of the central dogma to his thesis. I shall try to explicate my reasons for believing this.

From a biochemical standpoint, the information transfers barred by the central dogma, while being highly improbable from both empirical and theoretical standpoints, are nevertheless conceivable in terms of the principles of enzymology.[7] Consider, then, a system in which the transfer, DNA ⟶ protein ⟶ DNA, actually did take place. (There would be a net loss of information in the second step, but this does not invalidate the argument.) In such a system proteins could act not only as the functional products of genes but also as genes themselves. They would be able to evolve independently of DNA and then pass their new sequential information back to DNA. Putting aside matters of control, integration and fidelity of information preservation (which would raise considerably greater technical problems than in the central dogma-based system) there is no reason why the evolution of proteins would then be any more Lamarckian than it is in organisms based on the central dogma system. The chemical events (transpeptidation, etc.) leading to changes in protein structure would be no less fortuitous than are the events leading to mutations in DNA. And the only conceivable way—on the basis of current paradigms of science—whereby the ordered complexity characteristic of biological macromolecules could arise independently of an intelligent agency (such as man) would still be through the process of natural selection. The molecules would have to be parts of a self-reproducing system, and the directiveness needed for their evolution would have to be imposed by the requirement that they contribute to the functional integrity and propagation of the system as a whole ("system" here denoting not only an organism and its parts but also the species and ecosystem of which the organism is a part).

There is another, related reason why a system in which the

central dogma is contravened would be no more competent as a basis for Lamarckian behaviour than one embodying the central dogma. As we have already seen, the genetic information of an organism is more analogous to a set of algorithms or instructions than to a simple blueprint. Individual genes must be looked upon as having more than one teleonomic function, and it is rare that even the primary teleonomic function of a gene (as, e.g., the catalytic activity of a protein enzyme) corresponds to a particular character state of an organism (an example of such a case would be brown eye colour). This consideration would apply just as much to our hypothetical system, contravening the central dogma, as it does in the known system in which the central dogma operates.[8] If, then, there were to be a generalised type of feedback from character states to the genetic complement responsible for those character states (as would have to be the case for a Lamarckian effect to operate) it would have to be from many character states to many genes and groups of genes—an even more inconceivable process than would be feedback from one character state to one gene. In conclusion, then, it is difficult to see how contravention of the central dogma would facilitate the operation of purposive effects in evolution.

2. Certain types of purposive-like effects are compatible with current concepts of genetics, and these are no less conceivable in the central dogma-based system than they would be in a system in which the central dogma was contravened. It is well known that computer programmes can be designed to modify themselves in response to challenges, and there is no *a priori* reason why the same should not happen with the DNA programme. Indeed, we have an excellent precedent in the immune response of higher organisms: protein molecules are specifically tailored to fit antigens, some of which the organism —and even the species—may never have encountered before. According to the most plausible current model,[9] this is accomplished by the generation of a large number of new DNA sequences (within certain structural limits) during epigenesis, and the subsequent selection of those sequences which code for proteins having specific combining activities towards the new antigens. The process takes place through an intricate system

[8] Indeed, a case might be made for the proposition that the occurrence of many: many relations between genes (or other forms of coded information and the primary products thereof) and character states is an essential prerequisite for the occurrence of self-reproducing automata and organisms, regardless of the details of the system upon which they are based.

[9] J. D. Watson, *Molecular Biology of the Gene*, 2nd ed. (Benjamin: New York, 1970), p. 581.

in which a large number of different antibody-producing cell lines evolve during epigenesis, and those lines with antibodies active against a given antigen are stimulated to proliferate in presence of that antigen. On a micro-scale the evolution of antibodies in an organism can be looked upon as taking place by a process of natural selection among cells, while on a macro-scale the direction of the process is governed by the needs of the organism. Here, then, we have a teleonomic process in an organism which involves changes in the organism's own, "invariant", fortuitously mutating DNA molecules.

Antibody production is a form of adaptivity that has evolved to meet certain types of challenge. It is not Lamarckian even though new genes are formed, because they do not get into the germ line. However, there is no *a priori* reason why the inheritance of acquired characters should not take place—within limits—in organisms based on the central dogma as well as in other organisms. While it is improbable, though conceivable, that specific antibody genes can be incorporated into the genome of the germ line, it is perhaps a serious possibility that there are, in the genomes of some species, key sites that are susceptible to being switched into two or more alternative states in response to certain environmental challenges. Moreover, there is no reason why such switching should not involve controlled changes in the nucleotide sequences of the germ line as well as in other cells of the organism. This type of system could confer adaptive advantages on a species and might arise through natural selection.

Such systems would be capable of modifying the genome only in localised regions and in highly restricted ways. They would be only pseudo-Lamarckian and would act teleonomically only in response to challenges to which their predecessors had been exposed in the past (which had led to the emergence of the systems). The response of such a system to a *new* type of challenge would be fortuitous: it might be favourable—and form the basis for emergence of some new character or even species—or it might be unfavourable. Such considerations would apply equally to a system in which the central dogma was contravened.

3. Regardless of whether or not such specific types of pseudo-Lamarckian effect take place, the enlarged-view of natural selection taken today by Waddington and many other biologists includes the recognition that generalised types of pseudo-lamarckian effects occur in evolution through a process known as *genetic assimilation.* In higher

organisms there is evolution of behaviour (passed on by learning) as well as evolution of the genome, and new forms of behaviour exert new selection pressures, thus having directive effects on genetic evolution. The directive effects which such selection pressures exert on genes during evolution of species are in a sense analogous to the directive effects exerted on the evolution of antibody genes in individual organisms through the immune response: in both cases a directive process is superimposed on "invariant", fortuitously mutating DNA molecules. The process of genetic assimilation can be self-reinforcing, leading to rapid spurts in evolution, as for instance in the emergence of the human brain. Such processes show that in evolution there is a relationship of continuing interplay between teleonomy and invariance, rather than dominance of one over the other, and such interplay is no less likely to occur in organisms based on the central dogma system than it would be in organisms based on other systems.

I have tried to show that Monod's chemical arguments regarding teleonomy, invariance and evolution do not stand up to close scrutiny. The criticisms I have made do not controvert Monod's basic position with respect to natural selection—indeed in a sense they support it—but they do expose certain flaws in Monod's conceptual framework, and in doing this they bring out the need to modify his interpretation of biology in certain significant ways.

*Nativism*

An illustration of the way in which Monod's interpretation of biology has socially relevant implications is provided by his views on behaviour and language. Again Monod shows a predilection to give primacy to the molecular level. Here it comes out in the form of *nativism*, i.e., the view that behaviour is determined by genetic inheritance rather than by environmental influences. He believes that even the deep structures of our language, thought and cognition are determined genetically: they correspond to our brain structure, and this is determined by the structure of our DNA. Monod is on very shaky ground here. As we have seen, epigenesis is not entirely autonomous. There is an environmental component involved, and this becomes of especial importance in man. There is no need to emphasise the impact of early experiences and cultural influences on the individual. If we are going to suppose that the structure of our thought and behaviour corresponds in some way to the structure of our brains, then we must also reckon that the structure of our brains is partly determined by environmental influences —and these are of a most complex and subtle nature. The failure to appreciate this can lead to serious misjudgments in sociology, medicine and elsewhere.

*Metaphysics*

Up to this point I have tried to show that Monod's attempts to *prove* the validity of Darwinism through arguments based on molecular biology will not stand up to close examination; and that in so far as molecular biology does support Darwinism, it is in a global rather than a detailed sense. I have also suggested that Monod's analysis of the bearing of molecular biology on evolution theory and psychology is distorted by an over-preoccupation with the molecular level, and a neglect of the importance and subtlety of the part taken by environmental factors in epigenesis. I now want to inquire further into the nature of Monod's basic, metaphysical position and its interrelations with molecular biology. The following extracts from *Chance and Necessity* provide a point from which we can proceed. Referring to epigenesis Monod writes:

> The determining cause of the entire phenomenon, its source, is finally the genetic information represented by the sum of the polypeptide sequences ... screened by the initial conditions ... (p. 94)
>
> ... personally I am convinced that in the end only the shape-recognising and stereospecific binding properties of proteins will provide the key to these phenomena. (p. 89)

Referring to the brain he writes,

> Nothing warrants the supposition that the basic interactions are different in nature at different levels of integration. (p. 140)

The position expressed in these extracts is a form of materialism which can usefully be thought of by reference to a principle termed micro-reduction by Schlessinger.[10] Adherents to this principle hold, roughly speaking, that the properties of a thing should be explained as far as possible in terms of the properties and relations of its parts. Micro-reductionism has a long intellectual history, dating back to the early

[10] G. Schlessinger, *Method in the Physical Sciences* (Routledge & Kegan Paul: London, 1963).

Greek atomists and receiving a strong impetus from the mechanical revolution of the seventeenth century. It was at the latter time that Galileo, Descartes and others set going what many consider to have been one of the most important underlying programmes of modern science: that of trying to explain everything (except, initially, mind and God) in terms of "matter and motion".[11–14] This programme raised major philosophical problems which have occupied philosophers ever since. One of these problems concerned the relation of *secondary qualities* to *primary qualities*, i.e., of those "qualities" which we experience, such as colour and smell, to those "qualities" in terms of which all phenomena were to be explained, such as the number, shape and motion of particles. Seventeenth- and eighteenth-century disputes over primary and secondary qualities now take the form of disputes over the nature of mind, and over various forms of reductionism and anti-reductionism. Does molecular biology bear on such issues?

Monod is right to hold that the concepts of information-storage in DNA, and of the expression of that information through the shape-recognising and stereospecific-binding properties of proteins constitute major advances in the micro-reductionist programme as applied to organisms. These concepts provide a model for the assembly of atoms into larger units, which have more complex and specific properties than atoms themselves, and can in turn act as a basis for the assembly of still larger structures and for dynamic, cybernetic-like networks. Prima facie, it might be argued that Monod's emphasis on genetic *information* is a move away from micro-reductionism, since he seems to give information an almost independent, ontological status. I do not believe that this would be a correct interpretation of Monod's position or of reductionism as it is understood by contemporary philosophers of science.[15] In Schlessinger's formulation[10] "information" would come under the category of "relations of its parts"—in the present case those parts being the amino acid and nucleotide residues of proteins and nucleic acids. And, more generally, the role of "information" in the conceptual framework of molecular biology would be to

[11] A. N. Whitehead, *Science and the Modern World* (Macmillan: London, 1925; also Mentor paperback).
[12] E. A. Burtt, *The Metaphysical Foundations of Modern Physical Science*, 2nd ed. (Routledge & Kegan Paul: London, 1932; also Anchor paperback).
[13] A. Koyré, *Metaphysics and Measurement* (Chapman and Hall: London, 1968).
[14] M. B. Hesse, *Forces and Fields* (Nelson: London, 1961).
[15] E. Nagel, *The Structure of Science* (Routledge & Kegan Paul: London, 1961), Chapters 11 and 12.

act as a common denominator of molecular genetics and macromolecular biochemistry, and hence contribute towards bridge principles for the reduction of genetics to chemistry (a reduction that is still far from having been achieved in either a biological or a philosophical sense).[16, 17]

One way in which Monod goes wrong is to want to make universal principles out of current concepts of molecular biology, instead of regarding them as part of an evolving explanatory model. There is no logical justification for his supposition, that sequential information in DNA is the *sole* repository of hereditary information, that the specific properties of proteins are the *sole* means of expression of the information in DNA, or that the basic interactions are *all* the same at different levels of integration. Thus, there remains a distinct possibility that hereditary information in higher organisms may be carried not only in nucleic acids but also in other informational structures or systems.[7] And, as we have already seen, genetic information in DNA is expressed not only through stereospecific-binding properties of proteins but also through properties of RNA and of DNA itself. Finally, there is no compelling reason for supposing that basic interactions are the same at all levels of integration—though it may be a fruitful research strategy to assume that they are, until conflicting evidence turns up. The conceptual framework of molecular biology should be regarded not as representing "concrete truth" but, rather, as constituting an evolving model for the explanation of certain characteristics of living organisms in terms of molecular structures and interactions. At best it provides a framework for the integration of limited aspects of current biological knowledge, and leading principles for the guidance of further investigation; at worst it becomes the basis of a new dogmatism.

Micro-reductionist analysis should not be thought of as excluding other forms of analysis. Thus, a significant and legitimate role is also played in science by what Schlessinger has called *macro-reduction* (ref. 10, p. 56), i.e., the principle of explaining things *functionally* in terms of wholes of which they are parts. Macro-reductionist analysis can be found both in the physical and the life sciences. In biology, for instance, scientists who deal with cell biology or development tend to think of proteins in terms of their functions in the overall economy of cells, tissues or organisms: chemical mechanisms underlying the

[16] E. Nagel, *Journal of the History of Biology*, *2*, 128 (1969).
[17] D. L. Hull, *Philosophy of Science*, *39*, 491 (1972).

functions of proteins are of no particular interest to them, since all they need to know is that a given protein functions in such and such ways. These scientists are macro-reductionist with respect to proteins, but they are micro-reductionist with respect to higher levels of organization. In contrast, other scientists, such as X-ray crystallographers, are primarily interested in explaining the functions of protein molecules in terms of their underlying fine structure. These scientists are micro-reductionist with respect to proteins, but macro-reductionist with respect to atoms. As Schlessinger and others [15, 18, 19] have pointed out, there is no reason to consider micro- and macro-reductionist explanations of a given phenomenon as being incompatible with one another: rather, they should be considered as being complementary. Interrelations between micro- and macro-reductionist forms of explanation are, perhaps, best thought of in terms of hierarchical systems (as discussed by other contributors to this volume).

*Possibility of biological revolutions*

So far my criticisms of Monod's scientific position have been relatively superficial. I have questioned certain of his interpretations of molecular biology but not the basic, metaphysical presuppositions of molecular biology itself, upon which my own as well as Monod's interpretations have been based. The possibility remains that at some time in the future more radical modifications to our interpretations of biology will be brought about through scientific revolutions affecting the basic metaphysical presuppositions themselves.

Many molecular biologists, including Monod, would vigorously oppose the idea that their most basic postulates may one day have to undergo radical revision. They realise that there are large ranges of phenomena as yet unexplained, but these are looked upon more as gaps to which present concepts are in principle extendable rather than as possibly representing phenomena of a really unknown nature. And even if the latter possibility is admitted, it is assumed that the types of new insight which such phenomena might lead to could simply be added to (or superimposed upon in a simple way) the securely achieved insights of current molecular biology, rather than that they might entail radical reassessment and reinterpretation of

[18] M. Beckner, *The Biological Way of Thought* (Univ. Calif. Press: Berkeley and Los Angeles, 1968).
[19] W. Wimsatt, *Studies in History and Philosophy of Science*, *3*, 1 (1972).

current concepts. Conservative attitudes of this type predominate in periods of *normal* science, and only when serious anomalies arise and a *revolutionary* situation is generated do scientists begin in earnest to explore their basic presuppositions.[20] At present molecular biology and related biosciences are still in a phase of rapid and successful expansion, i.e., normal science, but this does not mean to say that serious anomalies may not arise in the future. It cannot be over-emphasised that our ignorance of organisms is still vast compared with our knowledge of them. In the areas of biogenesis, epigenesis and mental function, as Monod himself admits, we have as yet only the barest rudiments of comprehensive models.

An essential characteristic of scientific research in its more revolutionary aspect is that the scientist is searching for the unknown or, in other words, that he does not know what he is searching for. Revolutions have abounded in the past evolution of science, and there is no reason to think that they will not continue to occur in the future. However, one cannot foretell what form such revolutions will take; one can only look for possible pointers and make guesses.

One direction in which revolutions might, perhaps, take place concerns the micro-reductionist approach of trying to analyse all the properties of organisms in terms of their parts—in particular their molecules. It is difficult for one steeped in the traditions of modern biology to conceive of phenomena that would radically resist analysis in such terms. However, in twentieth-century physics micro-reductionist explanation has broken down for phenomena associated with very small structures (elementary particles, atoms), very large structures (those of cosmology), and even certain intermediate-size structures (superfluids, the laser phenomenon, and quantum-co-operative phenomena in general). In view of such precedents, the possibility must be borne in mind that the micro-reductionist approach may also break down for some biological phenomena.

It remains to be seen whether or not this will actually happen. Brain research has not yet progressed far enough for a realistic judgment to be made as to the probability that mental phenomena will turn out to be explicable in micro-reductionist terms, and the view that they will be is more a matter of faith and of research strategy than of rationality. The same applies to embryology and development. A more

[20] T. S. Kuhn, *The Structure of Scientific Revolutions*, 2nd ed. (Chicago Univ. Press: Chicago, 1970).

direct challenge to the micro-reductionist programme is posed by bird migration, the phenomena of which are far less complex than those of brain function and development but have nevertheless stubbornly resisted persistent attempts at micro-reductionist analysis. A potentially even more radical challenge to the micro-reductionist programme comes from parapsychology, a subject not even mentioned by Monod in *Chance and Necessity* in spite of the counter-evidence it presents to his world view. Parapsychology is a field of increasingly active research, and even the mildest claims of parapsychologists, if veridical, would raise profound problems for the micro-reductionist approach in molecular biology (and in science generally). It seems conceivable, then, that even a broadened micro-reductionist conception of organisms, which is hierarchical and includes recognition of macro-reduction, might at some stage break down.

Micro-reduction is but one out of a whole complex of only partly defined presuppositions, underlying Monod's world view, which might at some future time undergo revision. There may be other, more vulnerable presuppositions, to which I and most other contemporary scientists are still quite blind. I have only dwelt at some length on micro-reductionism because it provides an illustration of what I mean by a potential revolution. The main point I wish to make in this connection is that deep revolutions are still very likely to occur in biology and that such revolutions may entail unforeseen changes in the ways we look at organisms—including ourselves.[21]

[21] I wish to thank the following for stimulating discussions on a variety of topics relating to this paper: E. W. Bastin, D. Bohm, G. Buchdahl, F. H. C. Crick, D. Emmet, M. B. Hesse, R. C. Lewontin and M. H. F. Wilkins. This work has been supported by grants from the John S. Cohen Foundation and another charitable organisation.

CHAPTER TEN

# *On the Subjectivity and Objectivity of Knowledge*

DAVID BOHM

From early times, man has realised, at least implicitly if not always explicitly, that knowledge has both a subjective and an objective aspect. This realisation has led to a tangle of problems and paradoxes that have not really been resolved or dissolved. Indeed, even today, arguments on this question, such as those appearing in Monod's *Chance and Necessity* are caught up in the same sort of general confusion that has characterised discussions on this matter for thousands of years. To answer Monod directly, point by point, on such issues would mainly tend to continue the confusion, rather than help to clear it up. So perhaps a more appropriate approach will be to begin by discussing Subjectivity and Objectivity in a rather general way. In the light of this discussion, perhaps we can later make contact with some of Monod's key ideas in such a manner as to shed light on the issues involved.

Now, the very word "subject" implies a person who is thinking of himself as having the power to *subject* the world, to an overall pattern of order and structure determined by himself. For example, the "subjects" of a king are, in this sense, to be regarded as people who are "subjected" by the king to whatever he wills. Young children generally pass through a phase of development in which they imagine a world in which everything is thus subjected to their heart's desire. Eventually, of course, they realise that this is not possible "in the real world" and so, in one way or another, they begin to admit the primacy of objective reality.

The words "objective reality" imply a world that stands on

its own, as a coherent and stable totality, which is entirely independent of whatever any conscious subject may think or desire. Although this notion has a certain simplicity that may attract us, it is evidently one-sided and inadequate. For the whole point of man's thought and practical activity is that, with its aid, he does not have to accept "objective reality" as inevitable, in the sense of being *entirely* independent of his thought and of his will. Rather, he may regard himself as an *active* subject who, being guided by his thought, can participate in the world, to change things in ways that make them fit his notions as to what is suitable for him. This activity is not only adaptive, but also creative. For man can have insight into new orders, new forms, and new kinds of possibilities, and can realise such possibilities through action arising from this insight. So, in some way, it is not adequate to look on reality being *nothing but* objective, i.e., entirely independent of the subject.

On the other hand, it is generally evident to mature people that the world is subject to the order and form in their thinking and in their will only to a certain limited extent. For the universe, in its totality, goes immensely beyond anything that could be thus subjected, even by the whole of humanity over indefinitely long periods of time. Now, in former periods, people became aware of this and were led to the notion of God, as the creative source of both nature and man. In this view, subjectivity ultimately dominates objectivity. Although the world of nature is admitted to have a certain kind of real existence, nevertheless, the order, form, structure and even the subsistence of nature are regarded as completely dependent on what can perhaps be called "God's creative thought, as manifested in His will".

As long as people could accept this notion, through their religious faith, there was in fact no problem as to the meaning of knowledge. For ultimately, all that exists was determined in conformity with "God's knowledge" which, of course, had to be total and perfect. Man could know reality only in so far as he could participate, necessarily incompletely and imperfectly, in this knowledge.

Although this religious view of the cosmos did not give rise to any insuperable problems as to the nature of knowledge, it eventually failed to make adequate contact with man's practical needs and with his curiosity about nature. Those who were interested in these latter fields continued to inquire into them in ways that were almost independent of their ideas about God. Indeed, they eventually began to regard the world as a mechanical system, similar to a clockwork, constructed and set in motion originally by God, and then allowed to follow its own course. And thus, tacitly and by implication, they began, in effect, to treat the world as "objective reality" in their practical and scientific work, while they continued to regard it as "God's creation" in their thoughts on how religious matters impinged on human affairs. With the coming of the modern era of commerce and industrialism, this dualistic approach began to dominate. It was given what is probably its most adequate philosophical form by Descartes. Descartes proposed that reality was constituted of two independent substances; these were *extended substances* (essentially matter moving mechanically in space and time) and *thinking substance* (essentially mind, which was without extension, but which moved in its own way in the activity of thinking, willing, etc.). Because the two substances were so different, neither had in it any basis for a relationship with the other. But since the profession of a religious faith was still the general rule in his day, Descartes was able to solve this problem by bringing in God who, being the creator of both substances, was able also to be the ground of their mutual relationship.

As time went on, however, religious faith became progressively weaker, so that eventually, in theories of the evolution of life and of the cosmos, men were able to think of the totality as self-existent, not requiring God for its creation or for its subsistence. In spite of this, however, scientists generally went on with the Cartesian philosophy, not noticing that without God, the two substances came apart and lost all basis for a possible relationship between them. As a result, the Cartesian philosophy fell into confusion, and gave rise to a host of insoluble problems concerning the nature of knowledge. For if mind is a thinking substance, possessing knowledge of matter, which is extended substance, then one has to explain *how* mind can know that with which it has no relationship.

In the pursuit of a solution to this rather unclear problem, the idea arose of ending the mind-matter duality by proposing that ultimately, only matter has independent reality. Thus, the tables were completely turned. Whereas formerly, matter was explained as the result of the creative action of something of the nature of mind, spirit, intelligence (i.e. God), now mind was explained as a result of the mechanical movement of matter. Nevertheless, those who proposed such views rarely understood how far they had come from their Cartesian starting points. For they were proposing that *everything* is mechanical, mind as well as matter. Whereas Descartes would have agreed that inanimate matter is mechanical, and that the cell, the organs, *seen as extended substance* are mechanical, he could hardly have gone so far as to accept the notion that the mind, too, is completely mechanical.

The attempt to reduce *everything* to mechanism leads to such confusion that nobody, not even the most extreme proponent of this view of universal mechanism, can actually adhere to it in *what he does* (even though verbally he may give assent to such a view). Consider, for example, a person who said (in accordance with what is implied in the main thesis of Monod's book) that everything was the result of chance and necessity, in the mechanical motions of the molecules, out of which all is constituted. It would follow from this that what this individual himself said was also nothing but the result of chance and necessity in the motions of the molecules out of which he was constituted. Likewise, another individual who had opposite views would be made to develop them and utter them, only through chance and necessity operating in the same way. The collision of views between these two individuals would then be nothing but an extension of the collisions of the molecules out of which they were constituted.

Evidently, nobody would in fact be able to act in harmony with such a view. Thus, even the individual who claimed that all was mechanical would have to assert that his views were *true* while his opponent's views were *false*. Nowhere in a mechanical description of molecules is there room for such notions as truth and falsity. Neverthe-less, the holder of mechanistic views would have to imply that an opponent who persistently fails to see the truth of the mechanistic position must somehow be deceiving himself. But what can it mean for a machine to deceive itself? And what can it mean for one machine to say that it knows that it is functioning to give the truth, while it knows that another machine of a similar nature is functioning falsely? A machine can only operate according to the unalterable mechanical laws of chance and necessity which govern its behaviour. Any attempt to account for truth and falsity in such mechanical terms must give rise to confusion without end.

Somehow, nobody can help but imply that he himself is at least in principle capable of apprehending and communicating a truth that is not merely an automatic and mechanical conditioned reaction to the stimuli that he experiences. And so, even while he asserts that all is mechanical, the holder of mechanistic views tacitly shows by his actual behaviour that he exempts his own mind or "innermost self" from this dictum (and by implication, that he exempts the minds of others to whom he is talking).

It follows from this that in any theory which attempts to base itself on the universality of mechanism, something very much like mind, spirit, intelligence, or even God, lurks in the background. This often shows itself in the assumptions that the speaker (and those who listen to him) have what amounts to an unlimited power of free choice, entirely unrestricted by the mechanism out of which they are supposed to be constituted, to determine their actions, their morals and ethics, and their highest values. This is not only a kind of roundabout and indirect assertion of the ultimate supremacy of the subject, but it is also highly reminiscent of the injunctions given by the religious authorities in the days when the acceptance of religious faith was the general rule (when people were warned, for example, that they must choose good and not evil). While it was perhaps consistent for Church authorities to do this, it is evidently highly inconsistent, and indeed, confused, for one who believes in complete mechanism to exhort people to make choices involving morals and ethical values. The most that he might do consistently is perhaps, to make *predictions* as to what people will do, if treated, processed, and conditioned in various specified ways.

Although this sort of inconsistency and confusion is mainly only implicit in what is said by those who believe in complete mechanism, Monod's book goes farther, and makes explicit what has been explained and described above. Thus, consider Monod's postulate of objectivity. (*Chance and Necessity.*)

> "The cornerstone of the scientific method is the postulate that nature is objective. Science as we understand it to-day needs the strictest censorship implicit in the postulate of objectivity —pure and impossible to demonstrate.
>
> At all costs we must recognise that science attacks values, and a radical distinction must be established between ethics and knowledge; knowledge in itself is excluded from all value judgments.
>
> But the 'first commandment' which ensures the foundation of objective knowledge, is not itself and cannot be objective. It is a moral rule, a discipline. True knowledge constitutes an ethical choice and not a judgment reached from knowledge, since,

> according to the postulate's own terms, there cannot have been any true knowledge prior to this arbitrary choice. In order to establish the norm for knowledge, the objectivity principle defines a value; that value is objective knowledge itself. To assent to the principle of objectivity is thus to state the basic proposition of an ethical system; the ethics of knowledge.
>
> The ethics of knowledge does not impose itself on man; on the contrary, it is he who imposes it on himself; making it the axiomatic condition of authenticity for all discourse and all action."

It seems to follow from the postulate of objectivity that Monod is, in effect, regarding man's moral and ethical choices as arbitrary, not determined by chance and necessity, operating in the laws of his molecular constitution. Of course, this is consistent with his Cartesian philosophy, in which mind and matter are regarded as entirely different substances. However, Monod does not appear to bring God into his philosophy and, as has been seen, without God, who would relate the two substances, the Cartesian point of view does not hang together. In another side of his work, Monod seems to recognise this, for he frequently seems to be saying that there is only one purely mechanical substance, ruled by chance and necessity, and implying thereby that mind must be of this substance. But if this is the case, then he will be caught in the insoluble problem described earlier of how one can regard his own mind as completely mechanical, without implying that what he says is no more than an automatic reaction to the stimuli that he experiences.

However, as indicated at the beginning of this article, rather than try to analyse all these unclear questions in great detail, it is better to go on with the more general discussion of the issues involved. Of these, the most important one is perhaps that of the extreme dogmatism, shared by Monod and by the religious authorities, especially in earlier times, when religion played a dominant role in human affairs. One could indeed regard the postulate of objectivity as a paraphrase of former articles of religious faith which people were required to accept as the only possible form of truth (i.e., in Monod's terms, authenticity of *all* discourse and action). To carry the parallel further, it was supposed by the Church that, if man is to be good, he must "freely" assent to God's will (as interpreted by the religious authorities).

In a rather similar way, Monod requires man's "arbitrary" assent to the principle of objectivity (perhaps to be interpreted by suitable scientific authorities). Both the religious authorities and Monod agree on the need for a strict "censorship" of views contrary to what is regarded as right and good. They both talk in terms of "commandments", and of the need for man to "impose on himself" whatever may be regarded as the right set of ethical principles and moral values.

In effect, Monod is proposing that objective scientific knowledge should replace religion, not only as a source of knowledge of the world, but also, as a source of authority which determines the whole of man's being, even his innermost feelings and aspirations. Before considering such a proposal seriously, is it not necessary to understand much more deeply than we actually do what is meant by objectivity, and to what extent man's scientific knowledge can in fact be completely objective; i.e., free of prejudices, opinions, conclusions and tendencies to self-deception?

We shall consider the latter of these questions first. Now, the generally prevailing scientific view (especially among molecular biologists) is that all is mechanical, not only inanimate matter, but also life. Thus, as Monod himself says: "The cell is a machine, the animal is a machine, Man is a machine." But is it actually a scientifically established fact that life is nothing but a machine? It is true that life has a *mechanical side*. Living matter obeys the laws of physics and chemistry. Molecular biologists have discovered that in the growth and reproduction of cells, certain laws that can be given a mechanical form of description are satisfied (especially those having to do with DNA, RNA, the synthesis of proteins). From this, most of them have gone on to the conclusion that ultimately *all* aspects and sides of life will be explained in mechanical terms. But on what basis can this be said?

In this connection, it should be recalled that at the end of the nineteenth century, physicists widely believed that classical physics gave the general outlines of a complete mechanical explanation of the universe. Since then, relativity and quantum theory have overturned such notions altogether. It is now clear that no mechanical explanation is available, not for the fundamental particles that constitute all matter, inanimate and animate,[1] nor for the cosmos as a whole (e.g. it is now

[1] See, for example, D. Bohm, *Foundations of Physics*, *1*, 359 (1971); also *Towards a Theoretical Biology*, *2*, an IUBS Symposium, edited by C. H. Waddington, Edinburgh University Press (1969).

widely accepted among cosmologists that in "black holes" there is a singularity, near which all customary notions of causally ordered law break down). So we are now in the strange position that whereas physicists are implying that fundamentally and in its totality, inanimate matter is not mechanical, molecular biologists are saying that whenever matter is organised so as to be alive, it is completely mechanical.

Of course, molecular biologists generally ignore the implications of physics, except when these implications support their own position. In this connection, it might be appropriate for them to consider that the nineteenth-century view of physics was enormously more comprehensively and accurately tested than is now possible for the current views of molecular biology. Despite this, classical physics was swept aside and overturned, being retained only as a simplification and an approximation valid in a certain limited domain. Is it not likely that modern molecular biology will sooner or later undergo a similar fate?

It seems clear that the notion that present lines of thinking will continue to be validated indefinitely by experiment is just another article of faith, similar to that of the nineteenth-century physicists. Rather than accept such articles of faith uncritically, it is surely necessary for us to ask whether those who propound them do so impartially and for entirely objective reasons. Or is there not a kind of "hubris" that seems rather often to penetrate the very fabric of scientific thought, and to capture the minds of scientists, whenever any particular scientific theory has been successful for some period of time? This takes the form of a fervently held belief that what has been discovered will continue to work indefinitely, ultimately to cover the whole of reality. Such a belief must clearly interfere with objectivity, since it keeps the mind "blinkered" and unable to look in new directions that might give evidence that the whole of reality is not as one likes to believe it to be.

What is need for unrestricted objectivity is a certain tentative and exploratory quality of mind that is free of final conclusions, which would imply the absolute truth of commonly held beliefs as to the nature of the whole of reality. With such a quality of mind, one can remain open and sensitive, even to the faintest hints and clues, indicating something new and outside the limit of current forms of knowledge. This implies, of course, that one be keenly aware of the ever present danger that knowledge in broad and deep fields may give rise to the sort of "hubris" described above, in which there is an unquestioned belief in the complete validity of current forms of thinking. This hubris not only tends to take hold of scientific thought; as history shows, in earlier times, it generally dominated the thinking of the religious authorities. If it is allowed to continue in science, this latter will in all probability eventually suffer the sort of decline of influence that has befallen the religious view of the world. (Indeed, there are already signs of such a trend, in the growing popularity of "anti-rational" points of view, and in the tendency for imaginative young students to keep away from the sciences, which many now regard as a straightforward and more or less closed subject, which is a dull, routine sort of affair.)

Particularly when one comes to such a deep question as that of the nature of subjectivity and objectivity, it is necessary that the mind be eternally open, free of dogmatism, and ready to inquire in new ways and in new directions. To have this state of inquiry is more important than the particular answers that may come out of such an inquiry. For each answer will just be relevant to an aspect or side of the question. It will be able to enrich our views on the question, without ever exhausting the essence of what is involved in it.

To finish this article, it will perhaps be useful to sketch briefly some of the views of the author. These are to be regarded, not as statements of final truth, but rather, as a further contribution to the unending inquiry discussed above.

Now, it is clear from what has been said thus far that much of the confusion around this question arises from the attempt to divide subjectivity and objectivity neatly into two separate and distinct categories, which are completely opposite and mutually exclusive. Or to put it more precisely, it is implied that everything is either subjective or objective and that this dichotomy covers all possibilities. However, as has been seen, the "objective world" is not completely separate from the subject, who through practical action guided by thought can participate in it and in certain ways, at least, change it to fit his notions as to what is necessary or desirable. When such action has taken place, the "objective world" is already different from what it was, so that it requires new observation and thought on the part of the subject, leading to new knowledge for him.

Of course, in many cases, this change may be neglected, and we may then regard the "objective world" as fixed more or less according to our earlier knowledge of it. But in broad and deep contexts, especially those which include society and the goals, aspirations, ethical principles, etc., of the individual, the change in objective reality produced by new knowledge can no longer be neglected. This can be put in another way by saying that the subject (which in principle includes the whole of society) can to some extent be treated as the object of knowledge. Thus, the sharp division of subject and object has broken down. The subject participates in an essential way in the object, and in fact *is* an essential part, side or aspect of the object. In other words, the subject has to be seen both as a cause and as an effect, within the total object of consciousness.

What this means in essence is that subject and object are to be regarded as two views of the one reality. Neither of these views can stand by itself as a totality, completely independent of the other. To a certain limited extent, nature can perhaps be looked on as completely objective, but in connection with any discussion of society and of ethics (such as that of Monod), the attempt to regard knowledge as completely objective cannot work at all.

What is needed more generally is to emphasise that knowledge is primarily a movement or a process, with two sides, objective and subjective. Any content that was on the one side will be found, in the next stage, on the other. While the two sides can be treated as separate for limited purposes, they both point to or indicate one and the same total reality. Thus, even with a simple material object, no single view can be identified with the whole of "what the object is". Rather, this latter is only implicit, and does not appear directly in any view at all. Similarly, the total object of our knowledge is also only implicit, and cannot be contained in either the subjective or the objective view.

When we understand this deeply, we may perhaps see that there is no point to the attempt to define the categories of subject and object once and for all, and that such attempts at definition cannot do other than introduce unresolvable confusion. So perhaps we will be able to be continually observant, to see in each case where the ever-changing line between subjective and objective falls, and where there is no line at all, but rather, a merging of the two in an unbroken and undivided movement. A moral and ethical development can then follow, which is not laid down as an arbitrary choice to be imposed by each person on himself, but which is rather the outcome of an unending, intelligent perception by each individual of the total situation in which he lives.

CHAPTER ELEVEN

# *Two Contrasting World Views*

THEODOSIUS DOBZHANSKY

Teilhard de Chardin and Monod have little in common, but this little is notable. Both achieved eminence in their respective fields of science; neither confined himself to his speciality; both endeavoured to build coherent world views, and to present the fruits of their endeavours to wide circles of readers in eloquent, even passionate, writings. But here the similarity ends. Their world views are irreconcilable. Teilhard embraced the whole range of human experience—scientific, philosophical, esthetic, religious and mystical—in one coherent world view. Monod casts out all religion, all philosophy (except his own) and much else besides. Not unexpectedly, he attacks Teilhard, and does so with extraordinary bitterness. This makes one wonder: may it be that the attacker feels deep down that his world view fails to provide a purpose for living and an escape from feelings of emptiness and futility? The Teilhardian synthesis is, to many people, more successful in these respects.

The narrower focus is advantageous to Monod, and the very wide one disadvantageous to Teilhard. There are different manners of exposition and argumentation accepted among scientists, philosophers, theologians and poets. Teilhard did not keep his science, his religion, and his mysticism in separate compartments, because his synthesis obliged him to relate these to each other. Thus he collided with the different mores of the respective professions, and was severely criticised from all sides.

As the following quotations show, evolutionary biology is pivotal in Teilhard's as well as in Monod's views. "Is evolution a theory, a system, or a hypothesis? It is much more—it is a general postulate to which all theories, all hypotheses, all systems must henceforward bow and which they must satisfy in order to be thinkable and true. Evolution is a light which illuminates all facts, a trajectory which all lines of thought must follow. This is what evolution is" (Teilhard). And: "no other science has quite the same significance for man; none has already so heavily contributed to the shaping of modern thought, profoundly and definitively as it has been every domain—philosophical, religious, political—by the advent of the theory of evolution" (Monod). However, the two authors view the evolutionary process in quite different perspectives.

The crucial issue turns out to be whether evolution is going in some direction, or it is a senseless happenstance. Teilhard had "a conviction, strictly undemonstrable to science, that the universe has a direction and that it could—indeed if we are faithful it should—result in some sort of irreversible perfection". To Monod, all ideas of this kind are anathema; they are signs of "animism". Primitive man, as well as Leibnitz, Hegel, Spencer, Marx, Engels and Teilhard, are dumped on the animist heap. Not to be an animist you have to accept as an axiom that evolution has no direction. Nature is "objective", not "projective". Monod sees "pure chance, absolutely free but blind, at the very root of the stupendous edifice of evolution". Most important is that "man knows at last that he is alone in the universe's unfeeling immensity, out of which he emerged only by chance".

The problem of direction or "necessity" *v.* "chance" deserves most careful consideration. It can, I believe, be shown that this dichotomy, applied by Monod to biological as well as to human evolution, is spurious. Evolution is neither necessary, in the sense of being predestined, nor is it a matter of chance or accident. It is governed by natural selection, in which ingredients of chance, and antichance are blended in a way which makes the dichotomy meaningless, and which renders evolution to be a creative process. During his long career as investigator and thinker, Teilhard's views concerning the role of natural selection in evolution changed a great deal. In his early years (including the time when *The Phenomenon of Man* was written) it seemed to him that natural selection involves too much "chance". He espoused orthogenesis instead. However, in one of his late writings he concluded that "One may say that until the coming of man it was natural selection that set the course of morphogenesis and cerebration, but that after man it is the power of invention that begins to grasp the evolutionary reins". Not many modern evolutionists will take exception to this statement. Writing a quarter of a century after *The Phenomenon of Man* had been written, Monod obviously has the advantage of familiarity with the advances of biology during this period. And yet he misconstrues the way natural selection operates.

Evolution is a theory which asserts that "The current state of a system is the result of a more or less continuous change from its original state" (Lewontin, 1968). Cosmic or inorganic, biological, and human or cultural evolutions are parts, or facets, or phases of one grand universal evolutionary process. It took cosmic evolution several billion years to generate life, and some further billions for biological evolution to produce man. In this sense, evolution has been directional (though not necessarily directed). It is not unreasonable to say that the evolution on earth has "progressed" from inert matter to life, to consciousness, to self-awareness. Whether evolution anywhere in the universe is bound to go through a similar sequence of stages is quite another problem. Teilhard seems to have come close to such a view; I see no compelling evidence in its favour.

Biological evolution can be viewed in its general or in its particular aspects (Dobzhansky, 1968). The most ancient living beings preserved in fossil condition were prokaryotes, like blue-green algae and bacteria. Eukaryotes came later, first invertebrates, then vertebrates, and man was the latest arrival. Viewed as a whole, the general evolution is directional and progressive. This conclusion is inevitable whether one examines the morphological complexity, or the advancement of sense organs, or of nervous systems, or brains. In contrast to this, particular evolutions, i.e., the evolutionary histories of various groups and lineages of organisms, do not uniformly show either directionality of progress. Many primitive forms coexist on our time level with most advanced ones; this signifies evolutionary stasis rather than progress. Others, notably some parasites, underwent regressive evolution. The commonest finale in most evolutionary lines is extinction, a fact with which Teilhard the paleontologist was quite familiar. And yet, progress did occur in some evolutionary lineages, among which that culminating in man is most notable, but certainly not the only one. The key to understanding of these evolutionary patterns is neither chance nor necessity. It is natural selection.

Teilhard's interests, at least in his philosophical writings, were centred almost exclusively on general evolution. He was deeply impressed by its directionality. He thought that orthogenesis, rather than natural selection, is called for as an explanation. He wrote that "without orthogenesis life would only have spread; with it there is an ascent of life that is invincible". Yet orthogenesis is a theory that ascribes evolutionary changes simply to unfolding of pre-existing rudiments; evolution was somehow predestined from the beginning of life to proceed as it did. If so, nothing really new is created or can ever appear. But predestination was a tenet uncongenial to Teilhard. Why should one spend billions of years moving towards Omega, why not have it created at once? Rather inconsistently with his professed belief in a necessity of orthogenesis, Teilhard described the course of evolution as "groping". He believed that "groping is directed chance. It means pervading everything so as to try everything, and trying everything so as to find everything". To a modern reader, "groping" is a most apt metaphorical description of evolution by natural selection. "Groping" may end in a fall from a precipice; it may also lead to discovery of new ways of life. And towards the end of his life, Teilhard, as quoted above, concluded that until man appeared the course of evolution was being set by natural selection.

In contrast to Teilhard, Monod relishes chance—"absolutely free but blind". Where does this free but blind chance reside? Mutation is the source of raw materials for evolutionary changes. Without mutation evolution would eventually cease (although failure of some ancient lineages to evolve for long periods of time was apparently not due to dearth of mutations). Mutation is unpredictable, except in a statistical sense. Presumably every gene has a certain finite probability to undergo a given kind of mutational change, although we cannot predict which particular gene will mutate, or where, or when. Unpredictability must not be confused however with a causality. It is often stated or implied that a gene can mutate in any direction. This is liable to be misunderstood. A gene can mutate in many ways but not in an infinite number of ways. Its mutational repertory is set by its structure, which is in turn a product of its evolutionary history. Thus, a gene coding for hemoglobin can mutate to another hemoglobin variant. It cannot be converted by a single mutation to a gene coding for myoglobin or for a cytochrome. It tends to conserve its historically evolved organisation.

The chance in mutation is blind, but it is neither "pure" nor "absolutely free". The situation is more subtle and more interesting.

The biological meaning of chance is that mutations happen regardless of whether they will be useful to the species when they occur, or ever. What is even more important is that the process of mutation supplies raw materials for evolution, but it does not by itself constitute evolution, any more than a pile of building materials constitutes a habitable house. Evolution is constructed from mutational materials by natural selection. There is a danger in over-simplification of our ideas about how natural selection acts.

Explicitly or implicitly, natural selection is often misrepresented as a kind of biological sieve: it retains good mutants, and lets deleterious ones to be lost. In some situations the selection does act in this way. For example, an antibiotic added to a bacterial culture may let all cells die, except a tiny minority which have acquired by mutation a resistance to this antibiotic. Being a biochemist and micro-biologist, Monod is inclined to envisage natural selection according to the above "sieve" model. But genes do not act independently of other genes present in the same organism. A mutant may be harmful in combination with some genes, neutral with others, and favourable with still others. Biological success or failure are conditioned by gene patterns rather than by separate genes independently of others. Add to this the controlling action of the environment—a given gene pattern may be favourable in some but unfavourable in other environments.

Natural selection is an antichance agent. Its action does not however amount to necessity. Its outcome is unpredictable in the long run. This must be carefully explained in order to prevent misunderstanding. A single mutation is repeatable—it can arise again and again. Thus, if an inoculum containing a large enough number of bacterial cells is exposed to a certain antibiotic, one can be fairly certain that some resistant mutants will be encountered. But evolutionary changes involve emergence of harmonious combinations of many genes. The human genetic endowment differs from that of an ape certainly in many thousands of genes. Was the ancestor of the human species which lived in mid-Tertiary times bound to evolve into man? Not necessarily, and this is not because the same mutational changes may not have occurred at the same times in the evolutionary history, but rather because the selectional processes were not foreordained to occur as they in fact did occur. If so, is Monod right asserting that man has "emerged only by chance"? The problem is too subtle and complex to allow such simplistic solutions.

Natural selection is an antichance but not a rigidly deterministic agent. It does, as a rule, enhance the adaptedness of a species in the environments in which that species lives, or make it adapted to new environments. However, it should be kept in mind that in the biological world a species can achieve adaptedness to its environments in different ways. Life has deployed itself in several million species, rather than a single one. This is because there is a multitude of possible ways to make a living in the environments on our planet. In the same geographic territory one may find many species of grasses, or of Drosophila flies, or mice, or monkeys. They exploit different sub-environments in different ways. Mankind appeared neither by chance nor by predestination. It is a product of a creative process of evolution.

The problem of evolutionary determinism *v.* creativity causes difficulties to Teilhard as well as to Monod. Of course, these difficulties are, in a sense, opposite in sign. Finding chance unacceptable, Teilhard formulates a "cosmic law of complexity-consciousness". He believes that "It is the nature of matter, when raised corpuscularly to a very high degree of complexity, to become centrated and interiorised—that is to say, to endow itself with Consciousness". I am unconvinced that such a "law" exists. As was his habit, Teilhard was viewing the problem in the light of general evolution. Indeed, in many evolutionary lines there has been an increase in structural and behavioural complexity; in some, there developed at least rudimentary consciousness; and in one, the human line, there arose self-awareness or "reflection".

Yet in some lines we find simplification instead of complexification. Thus, viruses may be simplified or degenerate bacteria or cellular constituents. Or consider the plant kingdom: there certainly was complexification in plant evolution, but not even rudimentary consciousness has developed. All this goes to show that the direction of evolution in a given line is not predetermined. "Necessity" is tempered by what can only be called evolutionary opportunism, rather than "chance". Evolutionary changes that occur in a given species or population are those which are advantageous at a given time and in a given place. The cost of the opportunism may be a debacle—extinction. There is one thing that natural selection certainly cannot do—it cannot foresee the future needs of a species on which it acts. It is for this reason that paleontology discloses many more extinctions than progressive improvements, in the history of life.

Despite his professed belief in orthogenesis, Teilhard did not regard evolution predetermined. In trying to forecast future evolution he saw that "There is danger that the elements of the world should refuse to serve the world—because they think". His religious faith, not his paleontological research, made him trust that the danger will be avoided. Some of his statements may seem to imply a kind of attenuated vitalism; thus he spoke of a "secret complicity between the infinite and the infinitesimal". The following is however a quite explicit statement which abjures any kind of vitalism or "animism": "The phenomenon of growing consciousness on earth, in short, is directly due to the increasingly advanced organisation of more and more complicated elements, successively created by the working of chemistry of life." There is no disagreement between this and Monod's view that life transcends physics while obeying its laws. Monod goes even farther "What doubt can there be of the presence of the spirit within us? To give up the illusion that sees in it an immaterial 'substance' is not to deny the existence of the soul, but on the contrary to begin to recognize the complexity, the richness, the unfathomable profundity of the genetic and cultural heritage and of the personal experience, conscious or otherwise which together constitute this being of ours: The unique and irrefutable witness to itself."

The "animist" dragon whom Monod has resolved to slay resides in theories which "see in living beings the most highly elaborated, most perfect products of a universally oriented evolution, which has culminated, because it had to, in man and mankind". The key words in this statement are "because it had to". For it seems undeniable that living beings on earth (and for all that we know they may not exist elsewhere) are the most "elaborated", or advanced, products of universal evolution. Likewise, man is the most advanced product of biological evolution. Now, in what sense can one validly affirm, or deny, that evolution was predestined to produce all that it did, rather than something else? Unless evolution was acausal (which neither Teilhard nor Monod ever claimed), this can be solely in the sense of Laplacean universal determinism. But this is trivial; it only amounts to saying that evolutionary events have antecedent causes. The nontrivial problem is whether in all environments in which life is possible, evolution would proceed as it actually did—from prokaryotes, to eukaryotes, to multicellular organisms, development of sense organs and nervous systems, more and more capable brains, self-awareness, and in a remote future the Omega?

Arguments have been presented above to show that the general evolution (in contrast to particular ones) is directional or oriented. And yet, the determinism of evolution is limited, above all because adaptedness to the same kind of environments can be achieved in many ways. Only mankind is capable, or may become capable, of directing the evolution of itself, and of other species, according to a preconceived plan. The directionality and progressiveness of general evolution are surely not just happy accidents. They stem from the nature of living matter and of the laws of biology, first of all from natural selection. General evolution "had to" be progressive. This is just as remarkable, and if you wish mysterious, as, according to Einstein, the power of man-created mathematical concepts to describe natural phenomena. In this sense, what Monod calls "the ancient animist covenant between man and nature" is very much alive, and this is one of the central ideas of Teilhardian synthesis. Man does discover that there are some laws of nature that make biological and human progress possible, without however making it guaranteed to occur under all circumstances. Evolution is explained not by its eventual outcome but by nature's laws, which man tries to discover.

To say that life from the beginning had the potentiality of evolving as it did, and of eventually giving rise to man, is however another trivial statement. It tells us nothing more than that man, and other forms of life, have in fact appeared. Life had also countless other potentialities which have remained, and probably will remain for ever, unrealised. What kinds of living beings could have appeared but actually did not, we have no way of telling. The history of life, like human history, could have been switched on paths different from those which they followed in reality. Moreover, this could well have happened in environments not radically different from the actual ones. Repetition of *precisely* identical conditions, on the planet earth or anywhere else, is of course inconceivable. It is useless to speculate about "what might have been" if the evolutionary history would have been switched on different paths. But it is important to understand that there is a large gap between an evolutionary potentiality and its realisation.

Natural selection does not fit in the category of "necessity", nor does mutation fit in that of pure "chance", under any reasonable definitions of these terms (which Monod leaves rather vague). Evolution was from time to time, and in some lineages, progressive; at other times and in other lineages it was neutral or even regressive. The "animist covenant" may be said to exist in the sense that the possibility of progress in evolution is implicit in the laws of nature. But, to reiterate this point, the realisation of this possibility is not guaranteed. Natural selection restrains the turmoil of mutations and gene re-combinations, by guiding the organic variation into channels that are as a rule adaptive. Yet the multiplicity of these channels, and the opportunistic character of many of them, makes progress possible but not necessary.

Science deals most easily with what is repeatable and reproducible. In evolution, repeatability and reproducibility are restricted to only the simplest evolutionary events (such as obtaining strains of certain bacteria resistant to antibiotics). Evolutionary histories are unique and in practice not reproducible (except perhaps in "thought experiments"). Monod quite rightly admits, and even stresses, the uniqueness of the two evolutionary events of fundamental importance: The origin of life from nonliving matter, and of man with his symbolic language. I have called these events evolutionary transcendences. The statement that the potentialities of life and of man were present at the time of the "Big Bang" in the primordial matter is, therefore, true but trivial. More meaningful is Monod's statement, with which I agree, that "Life appeared on earth: what, *before the event*, were the chances that this would occur? The present structure of the biosphere far from excludes the possibility that the decisive event occurred *only once*. Which would mean that its *a priori* probability was virtually zero" (Monod's italics). The appearance of life and of man in the universe were utterly improbable events, and yet these events did happen. The laws of nature are such that life and man were possible, and they did appear. The "covenant" ("animist" or otherwise) does not, as I see it, mean that whatever happened, happens, and will happen in the universe, was and is *caused* by the final outcome (life, man, Omega). It means that the basic fabric of the universe is such that these outcomes were and are possible. They would be endangered if, in Teilhard's words, "the elements of the world should refuse to serve the world". There is no iron-clad predestination; the "covenant" can be abrogated.

Monod's central thesis is his principle of "objectivity". Science is based on "systematic denial that 'true' knowledge can be got at by interpreting phenomena in terms of final causes". This is true as far as everyday practice of scientific research is concerned. One gets nowhere by interpreting one's experiments, measurements, or observations in terms of what the world will be like in the fullness of time. For example, the increase of the brain size in human ancestry cannot be explained by the need to transform *Homo habilis* into *Homo erectus*, and the latter into *Homo sapiens*. Such an explanation cannot be either confirmed or falsified by any further evidence that could be gathered. An explanation should be framed rather in terms which could make it at least conceivably subject to test, such as selective advantages which larger brains conferred upon their possessors during the process of transformation. Only man can act to bring about future states of himself and of his environment which he conceives as desirable. And yet, could not the basic texture of the universe, which makes certain future, or "final", states possible, be gleaned *ex post facto* from "objective knowledge" achieved without prior assumption that these states may or must occur? Teilhard thought so, in contrast to Monod. What is known concerning past evolution, suggested to Teilhard certain extrapolations, such as the future evolution climaxing in the planetisation of mankind and the Omega. It is, of course, undeniable that in framing these extrapolations Teilhard's religious faith was, to him, the guiding light.

It is impossible to write books like Teilhard's or Monod's without going beyond the bounds of "objective knowledge", and revealing one's metaphysical, esthetic and emotional attitudes and sympathies. Teilhard's world view was frankly centred on his Christian faith. Monod's is just as clearly anti-Christian, and following the lead of French existentialists, particularly Sartre and Camus (although the former is not mentioned in the book). Hence, the book concludes with the twenty-one-page long chapter "The Kingdom and the Darkness". This is the climax of the fascinating book. Regardless of one's philosophical sympathies, one cannot fail to be moved by this cry of despair and anxiety, hardly relieved by an only faint and uncertain glimmer of hope. While the "nineteenth century scientism saw leading infallibly upwards to an empyrean noon hour of mankind, whereas what we see opening before us today is an abyss of darkness". Science turns out to be a destroyer of man's hopes: "By a single stroke it claimed to sweep away the tradition of a hundred thousand years, which has become one with human nature itself. It wrote an end to the ancient animist covenant between man and nature, leaving nothing in place of that previous bond but an anxious quest in a frozen universe of solitude." And yet we have unabated "The profound disquiet which goads us to search out the meaning of existence".

The glimmer of hope is seen by Monod in the "ethic of knowledge". It is here that Monod's admirable ability to present lucidly subtle and sophisticated arguments suddenly fails him. We are told that "any mingling of knowledge with values is unlawful, *forbidden*". Ethics and values cannot be deduced from knowledge, as so many scientific optimists (including some well-known biologists) vainly hoped. On the contrary, "ethics, in essence *non-objective*. is forever barred from the sphere of knowledge" (Monod's italics). And yet, somehow knowledge is based on ethics! According to Monod, "It is obvious that the positing of the principle of objectivity as the condition of true knowledge constitutes an ethical choice and not a judgment arrived at from knowledge. . ." There cannot be any true knowledge prior to this arbitrary choice. Now, if the choice is indeed arbitrary, then how much reliability and objectivity is there left in the "objective knowledge"? And are all ethics and values equally arbitrary?

In the last pages of the last chapter, Monod follows Teilhard's example: he embarks on extrapolation and prophecy. He finds that "The ethic of knowledge that created the modern world is the only ethic compatible with it, the only one capable, once understood and accepted, of guiding its evolution". In what direction is the evolution to be guided? It is in the direction of "real socialism", and of "really *scientific* socialist humanism". In what way will it be "scientific"? Can it be derived from "objective knowledge"? Ideologists of Marxian socialism, in Russia and elsewhere, told us thousands of times that their policies and projects are thoroughly "scientific". But Monod rejects them with a scorn almost equal to that with which he rejects Teilhardian ideals. I can only conclude that Monod owes to his many readers a more thorough explanation of his world view.

NOTES

Dobzhansky, Th., *Teilhard de Chardin and the Orientation of Evolution*, Zygon, *3*, 242–58 (1968).

Lewontin, R. C., *The Concept of Evolution*, in D. L. Sills (Ed.), *Internat. Encycl. Soc. Sci.*, *5*, 202–10 (1968).

Monod, J., *Chance and Necessity*, Alfred Knopf, New York (1971).

Teilhard de Chardin, P., *The Phenomenon of Man*, Harper, New York (1959).

Teilhard de Chardin, P., *The Future of Man*, Harper & Row, New York and Evanston (1964)